MERRIE ENGLAND

The Medieval Roots of the
Great British Pub

Ted Bruning

A Bright Pen Book

Copyright © Ted Bruning 2014

Cover design by Ted Bruning ©

All rights reserved. No part of this publication may be reproduced, stored in a retrieval system, or transmitted in any form or by any means, electronic, mechanical, photocopy, recording or otherwise, without prior written permission of the copyright owner. Nor can it be circulated in any form of binding or cover other than that in which it is published and without similar condition including this condition being imposed on a subsequent purchaser.

British Library Cataloguing Publication Data.
A catalogue record for this book is available from the British Library

ISBN 978-0-7552-1670-3

Authors OnLine Ltd
19 The Cinques
Gamlingay, Sandy
Bedfordshire SG19 3NU
England

www.authorsonline.co.uk

About the Author

Ted Bruning has been a journalist in the licensed trade and brewing industry press since 1986 and was editor of the Campaign for Real Ale's monthly membership newspaper *What's Brewing* for eight years. Pub history has long been a fascination for him: his books include *Historic Pubs of London* (1998), *Historic Inns of England* (2000), *London by Pub* (2001), all published by Prion Books; *The Microbrewer's Handbook* (Navigator Guides, 2007), and *Golden Fire: The Story of Cider* (Bright Pen Books, 2012). He also has a BA (Hons) in Medieval History from University College, London.

Front cover picture: - the Crown, Chiddingfold, Surrey.
Back cover picture: - the Shaven Crown, Shipton-under-Wychwood, Oxfordshire

CONTENTS

AUTHOR'S PREFACE 7

INTRODUCTION 9

CHAPTER 1: ALE, DRINK OF THE PEOPLE 15

CHAPTER 2: WINE, MEAD, AND CIDER 31

CHAPTER 3: THE OLDE ENGLISH ALEHOUSE 48

CHAPTER 4: GUILDHALLS & MARKET STALLS 67

CHAPTER 5: ASSEMBLING IN TAVERNS 78

CHAPTER 6: TOWN & COUNTRY 103

CHAPTER 7: THE OLDEST INN IN ENGLAND 123

APPENDIX 1: INN SIGNS AND WONDERS 144

APPENDIX 2: DE LUDIS 149

APPENDIX 3: I WYLL YOW TELL A FULL GOOD SPORT 153

Further Reading 157

INDEX 159

AUTHOR'S PREFACE

In offering this admittedly slim volume, I am very conscious of being a pygmy standing on the shoulders of giants. The two giants who have particularly inspired me and, I know, very many others, are Peter Clark, author of *The English Alehouse: A Social History 1200-1830* (Longman, 1983), and Judith M Bennett, author of *Ale, Beer and Brewsters in England: Women's Work in a Changing World 1300-1600* (Oxford University Press, 1996).

Before these books were published there was a huge literature for lovers of pubs, like me, to collect and enjoy. But most (although by no means all) of what was readily available was either the work of Victorian and Edwardian antiquarians who, although vastly erudite, were neither rigorous nor reliable, or of amateur enthusiasts with no access to primary sources who were apt (and I include myself in this) to parrot what they had read without verifying it first.

The effect of Clark and Bennett's books was, it seems to me, to make the study of pubs and inns academically respectable as well as popular. There were, of course, academics working in the field before Clark and Bennett came along; but since the publication of *The English Alehouse* and *Ale, Beer, and Brewsters* there seems to have been an increase in the number of serious and deeply-researched studies to satisfy voracious appetites such as mine.

But there has always been one question left unexplored, perhaps because to a serious social historian it is rather a peripheral one: where did the pub – or more properly the alehouse – actually spring from?

There must have been a moment when there were no alehouses, and then a moment when there was one. When was that moment? Of course, it's unanswerable; but trying to pin that moment down has provides an excuse for an utterly absorbing trip through the social, political, economic, and not least the commercial landscape of Medieval England. Hopefully the reader will enjoy sharing the trip with me; hopefully, too, this book will prompt somebody better-equipped than me to make the same journey and return with a more detailed and conclusive report.

And that somebody will need to be first and foremost a specialist in local studies, like Judith M Bennett. Local records exist in vast quantity and are therefore a particularly fruitful field for searches of this nature; by the same token, they call for enormous resources of time and expertise and an affinity for interpreting medieval Latin written by people whose first language was not medieval Latin!

Finally, I gratefully acknowledge the help of one writer in particular. Martyn Cornell, author of *Beer: The Story of the Pint* (Headline, 2003), selflessly became my guide in tracking down stubbornly elusive primary sources: without him this book would have stalled long before it was even halfway finished, and I am eternally in his debt. My thanks are also due to Professor John Hatcher of Corpus Christi, Cambridge, and Professor Beat Kümin of the University of Warwick for their advice and encouragement.

Footnotes: as this book is meant for the general reader rather than the academic, I have decided to dispense with the distraction of footnotes and to indicate important references in the text instead.

INTRODUCTION

This is a book about peasants – medieval English peasants, to be precise, both rural villeins and urban burgesses; what they got up to when they weren't ploughing, sowing, reaping, and mowing; and, more particularly, where they got up to it. To be sure, ploughing, sowing, reaping, and mowing absorbed much of their time and energy. But they took the Biblical injunction that man does not live by bread alone (and, by implication, by the getting of it) very much to heart, if not necessarily in the way the Bible intended.

Thomas Hobbes's observation that life in a state of nature is nasty, brutish, and short is often pressed into service to sum up the life of the medieval English peasant – but wrongly. Hobbes's "state of nature" (*Leviathan*, 1651) was a state without government, embroiled in a perpetual war "all against all". "In such condition there is no place for industry," he said, "because the fruit thereof is uncertain, and consequently no culture of the earth, no navigation nor the use of commodities that may be imported by sea, no commodious building, no instruments of moving and removing such things as require much force, no knowledge of the face of the earth, no account of time, no arts, no letters, no society, and which is worst of all, continual fear and danger of violent death, and the life of man, solitary, poor, nasty, brutish, and short."

You could hardly come up with a greater contrast to the structured, regulated and above all communal life of the stereotypical medieval English village. Solitary? Maybe, for shepherds spending summer on the high pastures in the transhumant uplands of the North; but for most, quite the opposite. Villagers worked side by side in the strip-fields, carrying out the same tasks in the same way at the same time. They settled their disputes publicly in the manorial court, where they also served as jurors – not weighing evidence like today's jurors, but testifying as experts on the customs, geography, and characters of their communities. They worshipped together in the parish church, celebrated its feasts together, marched in its parades together. Poor? Most were, of course; but few were actually destitute, and there were always opportunities for a measure of advancement, even for the humblest, as a soldier or household official of the lord, in the ranks of the clergy, or among the senior grandees of the village. Nasty? Well, nastiness is hard to calibrate. Creature comforts were few for prince and peasant alike, and medicine was primitive at best. In fact the sufferings of the sick or injured prince who could afford medieval medicine were probably greater and certainly more prolonged than those of the sick or injured peasant who couldn't. But nasty? It depends on what you're used to. Brutish? If by that Hobbes meant random and violent, then no. Life on what amounted to a farming commune was highly organised, with little room for the enterprising individual to break ranks and throw into doubt the sure and predictable work of the season. Violent crime appears to have been rare, and although it has recently been argued that the murder rate was much higher then than now, medieval medical knowledge was so primitive that many assaults that would be trifling today were murderous then. Even in their sporadic internecine wars the nobility generally (but by no means always) spared the peasants on whom their income, after all, depended. And short? Well, the incredibly high infant mortality rate certainly kept average life expectancy down; but if you made it past 21 you had every chance of living to a ripe old age. Many medieval peasants far outlived their capacity to support themselves, and providing for them was a major preoccupation.

That isn't to say that peasant life wasn't hard. Farming without a single mechanical implement beyond the water-powered (and, from the 12th century, wind-powered) flourmill has been extremely physically demanding throughout the ages; and for the people who do the actual work the returns have never been what you'd call generous. To make the pickings even slimmer for the medieval peasant, much of his labour – two days a week or sometimes more – wasn't even for his own profit but for his landlord's: until cash generally replaced labour service at the very end of the period, rents and taxes were often paid in sweat.

You might argue that handing over 40% of your working hours in return for your home, your strips in the communal field, and the right to graze your livestock on the common is not excessive even by modern standards, especially as you generally got a fairly substantial lunch of bread, cheese, ale, and sometimes meat on the days when you worked for your lord. But on top of your labour service you owed a tithe to the church, and the lord had a formidable list of additional impositions as well. You paid a fee either in cash or livestock on every landmark occasion in your life: when you entered your tenancy, when you married, when your children married, when you died. There were also fines for every infringement, so one way or another you ended up enjoying very little of what you produced.

Not surprisingly, given the hardship of their lives, medieval peasants liked to party; and the Church saw to it that they had plenty of opportunity to do just that. Days off work – all of them – were owed to God and were therefore defended by the Church from encroachment by the lay hierarchy; and there were plenty of them. Sundays, of course, were sacred, when compulsory morning Mass was followed by a day of abstinence from useful labour for the purposes of spiritual and physical recreation. Then there were 34 Holy Days of Obligation (until 1777, when they were reduced to 10), which were major saints' days when the Sunday regimen was also in force – and if they fell on a Sunday, a weekday was earmarked for the "solemnity" instead. Each of these Sundays and Holy Days was, according to ecclesiastical regulations, preceded by a half-day off for spiritual preparation, giving the medieval peasant 129 days off per year.

There'd be another day off to honour the saint to whom the parish church was dedicated, and another if you were a member of a religious guild. That's 131 – three more than the aggregate of Saturdays, Sundays, Bank Holidays and annual leave enjoyed by the average British worker today. And that doesn't even count the short winter days when there wasn't much work to do and not much daylight to do it in.

These 131 days were, as we have seen, owed to God; and the pattern of divine worship followed by a lengthy period of quiet spiritual recollection would not be unfamiliar to the 17th-century puritan or the nonconformist of the 18th, 19th, and even 20th centuries. The big difference is that the devout observant of the modern period can occupy the Sabbath appropriately by studying scripture, whereas even the infinitesimal fraction of medieval peasants who were in any sense literate couldn't, because the Bible was only available in Latin – and even then, only to those who could afford to own a book: a luxury item in the days when every page, every line, every letter, was handwritten in a monastery scriptorium. How, then, to fill the empty hours after morning Mass?

Without wishing to undervalue the genuine piety of the times, these days off may have been religious in purpose but they were also the only opportunity the peasant had for secular activities both sanctioned, such as archery practice, and frowned upon, such as football, bowls, dancing, courting, drinking, and everything else that makes a life of toil worth living.

Already, though, we can see how different the social life of the medieval peasant was from our own. Of course there are obvious differences such as the general shortage of money and (not to be underestimated) the lack of artificial light. But the greatest difference lies in the communality of medieval life. More and more we tend to spend our spare time in the comfort of our own homes, taking pleasures that are determined for us by TV companies and games designers. Other than the necessities of eating and sleeping, the medieval peasant's home offered little inducement to stay in – not even so much as a chair with a back. The villagers took their pleasures together, as we shall see. But where did they go for their feasts and frolics? The village pub, perhaps?

Nothing seems more natural to us than the existence of pubs. They are the principal arenas of British social life. No soap opera would be complete without a local where the characters meet to advance or comment on the unfolding plotlines; and even if real life is no longer quite like that, we still take our pubs very much for granted. But there had to be a first one. So who originally had the idea of simply going out for a drink and a chat, and nothing more? Who originally had the idea of providing the amenities necessary to meet the demand? And which idea came first?

Perhaps at this point we should take a moment to decide what a pub actually is. No easy task, given that we are dealing not with a clearly-defined class of institution like a school or a church or a hospital, but with a continuum of different types of on-licensed premises in which the categories tend to blur into each other and in which each category is defined as much by what it isn't as by what it is. It may seem unnecessarily restrictive to try to construct a definition of what we intuitively know; but if we are to decide when pubs first emerged we have to have a fairly fixed modern type against which to evaluate the businesses and institutions of the past.

Broadly, we are talking about fully on-licensed, fully commercial businesses which are generally open, without charging membership or admission, to customers who need buy nothing more than a drink. This excludes clubs, which charge admission or require membership; restaurants, where a drink can only be bought with a substantial meal; functions suites, which may have a full on-licence but are only open to invited guests for special occasions; and village halls and community centres, which may also have full on-licences but are neither generally open nor properly commercial. Then there are hotels, which often have public bars. But a hotel is still not a pub even if it does have a public bar, and a pub is not a hotel even if it has letting rooms. The difference – which might be obvious to the onlooker but is undetectable in law, distinct inn licences having long been abolished – is one of purpose. The defining characteristic of a hotel is its accommodation, to which other facilities such as bar, restaurant, functions suite, and conference room are ancillary. The defining characteristic of a pub, however, is its bar. A pub might also offer hot food, live music, big-screen TV, and electronic games; but to the extent that these are ancillary to the main focus of the business, it remains a pub. Many pubs have, effectively, turned into restaurants; some have turned into live music venues. But if a customer can't arrive with the reasonable expectation of enjoying a drink and a chat and nothing else, then for our purpose, these are no longer pubs.

The question this book poses is simple: how far back do we have to look before we can see something that we would recognise as a pub? But if it's simple, it's still not straightforward. There are copious references to drink and drinking in various sources throughout the Middle Ages, even from Anglo-Saxon times, and many of them look at first glance as if they are referring to something we might call a pub. But context is all. To generate sufficient demand to sustain a viable pub there has to be leisure time; there has to be cash; and there has to be – that golden rule of business – consumer expectation: that is, people have to understand what the service is before they know whether they want it. Only at a time and place where all three boxes are ticked we can infer from often ambiguous, equivocal, and problematic references that a recognisable pub might actually exist.

CHAPTER 1: ALE, DRINK OF THE PEOPLE

The peasants and burghers of Merrie England had a surprising amount of leisure time on their hands, as we have seen, and plenty of diversions to fill it. As well as religious processions and pageants, there was music and dancing aplenty, physical sports such as quarterstaves and wrestling, gambling with dice and knucklebones, and more contemplative pastimes such as chess and backgammon. What psychotropic agent fuelled their festivities? Well alcohol, obviously. Not spirits, because distillation was scarcely known to them: the story of brandy, whisky, gin and rum belongs to a later era.

So ale, of course – there was always ale. Wine for the well-off. Cider, possibly; although as we shall see, that's something of a problem area. And, in declining quantities, mead. These were the drinks that made Merrie England merry. And since the life of the pub is predicated on the service of alcohol, we had perhaps better look at it first.

Ale was the favourite drink of the working classes across much of the world from that day in deep prehistory – maybe 8,000 years ago, maybe much more – when the miracle of fermentation was first discovered until the sad day rather more recently when someone put the kettle on instead.

Much has been made of the idea that peasants through the ages ordinarily drank ale because the water wasn't safe. Who first made this suggestion I don't know, but it is one of those ideas that has been repeated so often that it is now taken as hard historical fact. It has always seemed to me, though, to contain a fatal flaw: nobody knew that water that wasn't visibly polluted might actually be lethal until

1849 when a London doctor, John Snow of Soho, published *On the Mode of Communication of Cholera*. Until then – and for some years afterwards – the medical establishment believed that "miasma" or foul air caused the disease; and if the Victorian medical establishment didn't realise that apparently clean water might be infected, the peasant of ancient and medieval times certainly didn't. And as for medieval peasants shying away from water – well, the schoolboy in Aelfric's late 10th century *Colloquy* (that sagacious youth whom we shall meet a little further down discoursing knowledgeably about the wine trade) seemed content to drink water when he couldn't get ale; and four centuries later William Langland was complaining in *Piers Plowman* that many peasants were simply too poor to afford ale and had to make do with water instead. It is true that the monks of Blackfriars in London protested loudly and often (and apparently to no effect) about the state of the Fleet River; but given that the butchers and tanners of Smithfield just upstream customarily tipped their effluent into it, nobody with a functioning nose could have had any doubts about its potability. So: people did drink water. And there is no reason to suppose that the rural wells and streams that supplied it were particularly polluted anyway.

They preferred to drink ale (and often in considerable quantities) not for reasons of hygiene but simply because they liked it and knew it was good for them. Its fairly low alcohol content wouldn't have had much effect on their work once they'd developed a tolerance. Most journalists in the heyday of Fleet Street functioned with at least moderate efficiency after a lunch accompanied by far more alcohol than a medieval peasant would have seen in a week; and as the ale of yore was brewed without hops (which will only appear towards the end of our period), it didn't contain the soporific element that makes an afternoon's work after a few pints of modern beer so difficult to focus on. Despite its mild diuretic effect it still rehydrated the sweating labourer perfectly adequately. And – as today's dieter is well aware but the medieval peasant didn't consciously understand – it's a great source of readily-available calories (as well as B vitamins, although the medieval peasant can't have known that either). In short, ale was perfect for the needs of the pre-mechanised manual labourer.

You could say, though, that it was a miracle that such a perfect dietary supplement was ever discovered at all. The route from grain to glass is not a complicated one, but it's not an obvious one either. To achieve it, you moisten ripe grain in warm water until it starts sprouting. When little tops and tails appear you halt the germination process by drying the damp grain; then you grind it into a coarse flour or grist. This is soaked in hot (not boiling!) water to dissolve its sugars, and the sweet liquid or wort is drained off and fermented with yeast. The biochemistry behind all this is simple enough: when it's warm and wet, the grain thinks it's time to wake up and grow. So it produces an enzyme, diastase, to convert its load of insoluble starch into soluble sugar that will nourish the cornstalk until its roots are grown and it can feed itself. Just like an egg, really. By brewing up the crushed grain (which at this stage is called "malt") at a bit below boiling point you dissolve all its sugar and a whole load of other biochemicals as well, some of which are pretty tasty. The sugar in your liquid soon attracts a horde of microbes among which (you hope) will be yeast, a fungus that eats sugar and excretes CO_2 and – glory of glories – alcohol. This process is called fermentation, and when it's done – when the CO_2 stops bubbling up – you've got yourself a drink.

As I said, a simple process – but not an obvious one. Ologists of different schools argue, as they are paid to do, over how anybody ever stumbled across it at all.

The Origins of Ale

The origin of the malting stage is quite easy to fathom. The first farmers, in what is now the Middle East, stored their harvest in holes in the ground which cannot all have been entirely rainproof. Some if not most of the stored surplus got wet enough to start germinating. But grain was too precious to throw away, so our farmers rescued it by drying it in the sun or even over fires. Once they'd ground it into meal or flour they found it was sweet, because the enzymes had been prompted to start converting the starch in the grains into sugar – saccharifying, as brewers call the process. And since the human brain craves sugar because sugar is its principal fuel, the discovery was a very gratifying one.

But how and why this nice sweet flour was turned into an alcoholic drink is a harder question. There seem to have been two possible and similar methods; and for the following very potted history of brewing in the ancient world I am indebted to Martyn Cornell's *Beer: the Story of the Pint* (Headline 2000), and Dr Ian Hornsey's *History of Beer and Brewing* (Royal Society of Chemistry 2003). One idea is that some of it was baked into hard biscuit, perhaps for the use of hunters and merchants on their journeys, perhaps as a way of storing any surplus. To eat it they had to soak it, and their soggy leftovers started attracting those magic microbes and fermenting. Another is that some of the malt flour was used to make porridge, maybe to feed infants and the elderly and possibly flavoured and fortified with fruit, which carries yeast on its skin. Again, the leftover slops started to ferment, much to the delight of those who tasted it. Personally I prefer the latter theory, as it cuts out a putative process (the biscuit making) for which there seems little evidence; because leftover slops are more likely to be left standing around long enough to start fermenting in a village than among a group of busy people on the move; and because ale is still made this way in parts of Africa. Probably, both methods evolved in different circumstances. In later times, as we know from Ancient Egyptian wall-paintings, ale was brewed from water in which bread had been soaked. This method certainly works: it's been tried, and produced a pale, cloudy ale of about 5% alcohol by volume.

By the time the Ancient Egyptians and Meso-potamians invented writing in about 3000BC, ale had become a dietary staple for rich and poor alike, well-attested in both literature and public records and even governed by its own deities. But brewing had spread far beyond the Middle East. The first British ale we know of comes from about the same time – if, that is, the grooved ware pots often found on Neolithic sites were indeed, as archaeologists suspect, brewing vessels. Residues of what seems to have been prehistoric ale found in the Orkneys in 1929 contained pollens of hallucinogenic plants such as henbane and deadly nightshade: if this really was ale, it would have done a lot more than get you drunk! Perhaps it was meant only for shamanistic special occasions; but another apparent ale residue, found in a grave in Scotland and dating from about 1500BC, was flavoured with nothing more toxic than honey and meadowsweet (a preservative as well as a sweetener). By the time the literate world started noticing them, the Celts of both Britain and Gaul were ale-drinking people, as were the Germans across the Rhine. The Greeks and Romans may have preferred their wine, but the world around them was peopled with ale drinkers; and the Romans, ever adaptable, became (to an extent) ale drinkers themselves. Archaeologists have uncovered the remains of Roman-era maltings on a number of sites in Britain, and the Latin for ale, *cerevisia*, may even have derived from the Celtic *curmi*. Perhaps the ale was for peasants and legionaries while landowners and officers drank wine, most of it imported but some at least, as we shall see, domestic.

The Romans left Britain as they had found it: a land in which the usual drink of the common people was ale. As we have seen, the Celts liked to use honey as an adjunct – a practice attested not only by modern archaeologists but also by Classical observers including Posidonius in the first century BC, Pliny the Elder in the first century AD, and possibly even the adventurer Pytheas of Massilia. Pytheas actually visited Britain in about 320BC, and although his own works are now lost they were quoted by later writers and included a brief reference a beverage of grain and honey. It's also clear that the Celts favoured emmer, a strain of wheat, over barley as their principal brewing grain: some of the more adventurous modern brewers have produced honeyed wheat beers with great success, although as far as I know none of them have tried to replace hops as their flavouring agent and preservative with meadowsweet.

The Anglo-Saxons, who moved in almost as soon as the Romans had moved out, may not have shared much with the Christian and largely Romanised British Celts; but they did have one thing in common – ale. And evidently, they were brewers of some sophistication. From a range of sources as diverse as rent-rolls and leechdoms, Martyn Cornell has identified a dozen types of Old English ale including, from an 11th-century leechdom from Wessex, *Wilisc ealath* – Welsh ale, and so perhaps flavoured with honey. He also lists *hluttor ealu* (or, in the Anglian dialect, *hlutres aloth*), ale cleared by being left to settle or perhaps being fined with alehoof; *geswet eala* or sweet ale; *lithes aloth* or new mild ale; *strang hluttor eala* (strong clear ale); *hluttor eala wel gesweted* (well-sweetened clear ale;) *sur ealath* (sour ale); *niwe ealath* (new ale); *eald ealath* (old ale); *awylled ealath* (foaming ale, perhaps still fermenting); *twibrowen ealath* (twice-brewed ale); and *niwe ealo aer thon hit asiwen sie* (unsieved new ale). Some of these may be different descriptions of the same basic recipe; nevertheless, it is clear that there were different regional brewing traditions, different strengths, different ways of maturing ale, and different ways of flavouring it – which perhaps, given the ethnic diversity of pre-Conquest England and the changes and advances that must have occurred in brewing techniques over a span of some six centuries, is no surprise.

Ale in the Local Economy

The expertise of Old England's brewers both before and after the Norman Conquest (they were, after all, the very same people in 1067 as they had been in 1065 – an obvious point, but one which often seems to be forgotten) is a reminder of how important ale was to them. Not only was it a good source of calories and vitamins; it was a comparatively cheap one, too. Malt was far easier to get hold of than honey, the only other source of easily-accessible sugar known at the time. Ale was also, within limits, an item of exchange. Its bulk and short shelf-life (this was centuries before the preservative qualities of the hop were discovered) made it generally unsuitable for regular trading over anything but the shortest distances, but rents and taxes could be paid in it; and in time it was realised that it could be sold to other townsfolk or villagers, although it was not until after the Conquest, as far as we can tell, that brewing for sale became an important secondary income for many village households.

How ale got from the fermenting vessel to the drinker in pre-Conquest England is a different question, as we shall see; the Anglo-Saxons simply didn't think such mundanities worth recording. Such of their literature as survives is mainly made up of stern sermons, law-codes and canons, heroic ballads, and riddles. Minutely detailed records of grass-roots transactions were not the concern of the scribes of the day. The Normans were different. They were strangers in a strange land; and unlike the native thegns they displaced, the members of this new ruling elite were not intimately familiar with every field and fold, every copse and common, every croft and toft of the estates they had just won. To make sure they got their share, they had to write everything down. The Conqueror himself set the example, commissioning the Domesday Book towards the end of his reign as a village-by-village record of the assets of his realm; and it wasn't long before every manor in the land had its scribe, busily recording the day-to-day transaction of business, of justice, of rent, of tax, and of labour service that came to official notice.

Tireless research at grass-roots level over the last couple of decades has revealed just how many post-Conquest households sold at least some of what they brewed. Judith M Bennett in *Ale, Beer, & Brewsters* discovered that about a third of the households – ranging from the near-destitute to the comparatively prosperous – in the Midlands and

East Anglian villages she investigated were either fined or otherwise recorded as brewing for sale in the years immediately before the Black Death. Another study, of urban Exeter in the later 14th century, found almost three-quarters of all households brewing for sale. These ranged from occasional brewers who might sell the result of a single brewing to meet a sudden need for ready cash to what Bennett terms "by-industrial" brewers who brewed for sale regularly and obviously depended on the trade for a significant part of the household income. The Exeter study found nearly a third of households brewing for sale on a fairly regular basis. It should be noted that as brewing in medieval villages seems to have been exclusively women's work, the term "brewsters" would be more accurate than "brewers". Only in larger towns such as York or Oxford was there enough trade to sustain fully commercial brewing, and here the brewers recorded were more frequently male, although by no means always. In a village, it was scarcely possible to make enough profit from brewing to support any but the smallest families. Brewing was therefore almost always carried on by the wife of the household as a sideline or by single women as a livelihood; and even when men appear in village records as brewers, Bennett has shown that most of them were actually the husbands of brewsters, with other occupations of their own.

The Making of Ale

But what sort of ale were they brewing, these industrious women? The village inquisitions, sadly, don't tell us: their purpose was to count the pennies extorted from brewsters as fines for the vaguely-worded infringement of "selling outside the assize" (to which we shall return), which in time became part of the lord of the manor's customary rake-off. Court records, not unnaturally, don't go into detail about the nature of the ale that was being produced and nor, unfortunately, do our other main sources of information on the subject – monastery account books. Unless you lived close to a very important castle, the largest institution in your neighbourhood was undoubtedly the nearest monastery. Here the monks and lay brothers themselves, their workers and servants, inmates of dependent almshouses or hospitals, the abbot's guests, and travellers lodging at the *hospitium* (accommodating strangers being one of the charitable services monks had to provide) had to be fed and watered. A monastic brewery might therefore be a pretty big concern, the most famous and oft-quoted example being St Paul's Cathedral, whose brewery (as recorded in a surviving set of account books) turned out nearly 68,000 gallons of ale in 1286. (A medieval gallon, by the way, was much smaller than a modern gallon. The medieval pint was usually 12 troy ounces, against the 20 fluid ounce Imperial pint adopted only in 1825. A troy gallon, therefore, consisted of 96 fluid ounces, rather than the 160 ounces in an Imperial gallon. Seen in this light, records of nuns, children, members of royal households and so on swilling allowances of a gallon of ale a day are not quite as extreme as they first appear).

But while we marvel at the consumption by the monks of St Paul's and their various servants, employees, and guests of 1,500 pints of ale a day, we don't really know what they were drinking. We do know that the brewer, John de Braynford, used as much wheat as barley, and more oats than wheat and barley combined; and Cornell has calculated that the average strength of St Paul's ale would be in the order of 5-6% alcohol by volume. But de Braynford almost certainly didn't produce a single type of ale but a range of strengths and qualities for different occasions and for drinkers of different status. The best of it was fit for kings: Thomas Beckett, Henry II's chancellor, set off on a diplomatic mission to France in the 1150s taking with him among other gifts two cart-loads of ale that were, according to his secretary and biographer William Fitzstephen: "decocted from choice fat grain … most wholesome, clear of all dregs, rivalling wine in colour and surpassing it in flavour."

This wasn't the kind of ale being brewed for everyday drinking up and down the country, though. For one thing, Beckett's ale was brewed to withstand a journey by land and sea that will have taken more than a week. That means it must have been strong stuff, for alcohol is a great antibacterial even without the assistance of hops. By contrast, the alewife's regular brew was drunk as soon as it was sold, and needn't have been all that strong. In fact too much alcohol might not have been a good thing, under the circumstances: men drank while they worked, and their work often involved sharp objects such as scythes and pitchforks. Fitzstephen was also careful to mention that Beckett's ale was transported in iron-hooped barrels – after bacterial infection, oxidisation is ale's worst enemy and keeping the air out extends its life appreciably. The ale-wife's brew, though, was probably sold straight from the fermenting vat and never went anywhere near anything as expensive as an airtight barrel.

Another moderating influence on the strength of domestic ale was that thrifty alewives, it is universally agreed, commonly got two or even three mashes out of the same charge of malt; and just as if they had used the same teabag three times, each mash was successively weaker. The product of the first mash, it seems, was often held back for sale separately, even though the practice was illegal until 1276 under legislation that we shall examine later. The everyday ale therefore, was likely to have been a blend of the second and third mashes, of about the same strength as a modern-day session beer of 3-4% alcohol by volume. Alternatively, maybe some or all of the third and weakest mash was generally reserved for children, monks and nuns, and labourers with those dangerously sharp implements to wield, with the product of the second mash earmarked for more relaxed drinking after the scythes and pitchforks had been hung up for the day.

We might have a rough idea of how strong a medieval peasant or townsman's habitual drink was, and a better idea of what it was made of; we can't really know, however, what it can have tasted like.

The main ingredient of ale or beer was and remains grain (which is why saki is, technically speaking, not rice wine at all but rice beer), and the grain most commonly used by Anglo-Saxon brewers and their Old English descendants, it has always been asserted, was barley rather than the emmer apparently favoured by the Britons. But then at St Paul's, according to John de Braynford's account book, oats seem to have played a major if not dominant role in the grist of mixed ground malts. Oats are still used in brewing today, but as an adjunct rather than a principal ingredient: they seem to scrub the finished product to an unusual smoothness and are most commonly added to stouts and porters. What ale made mostly of oats (but with enough barley to supply the necessary diastase) would taste like I have no idea. However, most modern beer-drinkers will be familiar (or could easily familiarise themselves) with the characteristics of a beer brewed largely or partly from wheat malt, since several German and Belgian brands are now on sale in supermarkets and many pubs even stock them on draught. Unfiltered wheat beer is slightly cloudy, with aromas of lemon, cloves, and even bubblegum. British brewers nowadays commonly use a proportion of wheat malt in their grist to give their beer a lighter body and paler colour than all-barley beers, with a summery zestiness that challenges lager as a warm-weather beer.

After the variety and blend of grains, ale's most important ingredient was yeast. The action of yeast was not understood until well into the modern period; medieval brewers didn't know how it worked but were content that it did and didn't ask searching questions of it, often referring to it simply and fatalistically as Godisgood. Yeast propagation and the maintenance of true strains is one of the modern brewer's most assiduously conducted tasks, and breweries even have reserve strains kept in the National Yeast Bank at the John Innes Centre in Norwich in case their house strain gets an infection and they have to start all over again. How the medieval brewster kept her yeast safe from the infections to which it is notoriously prone is a matter for conjecture. Perhaps village brewsters swapped jugs of yeast among themselves to make sure there was always a live sample somewhere on the go; perhaps – as according to Martyn Cornell,

Norwegian country brewers did until a century ago – they dipped a branch of gorse into the foam on top of the of the fermenting beer, dried it, and dipped it again into the next brew. One thing we can be fairly sure about is that they didn't commonly, as some Belgian brewers do today, deliberately allow their mash to be infected by whatever bacilli and fungal spores colonised the seams of their fermenting vats or simply wafted in on the breeze. Lambic beers fermented by this apparently haphazard means have been made in and around Brussels since at least the 16th century – probably much, much longer – and are definitely an acquired taste. In fact, their rather agricultural flavour is often masked by the addition of cherries or raspberries. But although the medieval brewster might well have allowed wild fermentation to occur as a deliberate choice, she didn't actually have to. Yeast – or barm, or dross – is recorded often enough to know that she had at least some control over this most mysterious and valuable substance. Indeed there were some medieval drinkers who valued yeast highly enough to put the surplus foam from the vat to very good use: Ian Hornsey cites the tale of Franciscan friars who boiled up the sediment – mostly composed of *drest*, or dead yeast – from their ale until it autolysed: that is, until the cell walls broke down and the liquid thickened and turned, effectively, into Marmite.

Familiarity with modern beers, unfortunately, is no guide to the flavours of the ales of Merrie England thanks to one key ingredient of which English brewers of the time were entirely ignorant: hops. There is fragmentary evidence, mostly from 15th and 16th-century herbals and dietary tracts, that late medieval brewers and brewsters frequently flavoured their ales with a variety of herbs. Meadowsweet and ground ivy or "alehoof" (a fining agent with a bitter tannic taste) we have already met. What herbs the brewers favoured depended on the habitats in the neighbourhood: the aromatic sweet gale, for instance, grows in wetlands while the antimicrobial herb bennet or sweet avens prefers woodlands and hedgerows. Honey was also a favourite additive, producing Welsh ale or "braggot" (from the Welsh *bragaud*, meaning beer). If the honey were added to the mash before fermentation it would have strengthened and enriched the final ale; if a syrup of honey were added after fer-mentation it would have sweetened it. As to what these concoctions actually tasted like, however – well, it must remain mysterious. Many enthusiastic amateurs have tried their hand at recreating medieval brews (archaeologists have even recreated Egyptian and Mesopotamian ales); but their attempts are fatally handicapped by two factors.

The first is that the two basic ingredients – grain of one sort or another and yeast – have been so refined and altered in the past 500 years that we cannot know what a medieval strain would have produced. The second is recipes. It is just possible to reconstruct from account books and wills what an aristocratic or monastic brewhouse was equipped with and what ingredients were used. But the illiterate peasants who brewed most of the ale consumed every day left no records and, if they used herbs and honey at all, we have no way of knowing what quantities and proportions they used and how they used them. Approximate though enthusiasts' reconstructions might be, however, there are about 100 places in the British Isles, most of them in Scotland, where you might just be allowed to sample the direct linear descendants of medieval ales if you ask nicely. I'm talking about whisky distilleries. For the "wash" they brew as the raw material for their stills is nothing other than unhopped beer.

Hops and Beer

The use of hops instead of these herbs, once it became widespread, changed everything – the nature of the drink, the nature of the industry, even the language. You may have been wondering why we have been talking until now about ale, rather than beer. Not out of any intention to appear twee, to be sure: there is an actual difference. The word "ale" descends into modern English from the various Anglo-Saxon and Viking languages, while the word "beer" originates from German and Dutch. To any late medieval English brewer or drinker, "ale" would have been the native drink while hopped "beer" would have been a foreign beverage enjoyed by German, Dutch, and Flemish expatriates.

The hop, a climbing plant related to hemp and nettles, was a multi-purpose crop in early medieval times, used in brewing in many parts of North-western Europe since at least the early ninth century. The young shoots could be eaten (and still are in Belgium); the bine could be plaited for cordage or beaten into fibre to produce a strong yarn suitable either for sacking or finer cloth; the sap produced brown dye, while the leaves and flowers produced yellow; the leaves also made a digestive tisane; and the flowers or cones of the male plant yielded a strong soporific. But it was the cone's content of acids and resins that made it so attractive to brewers. The resins contain a range of flavours and aromas that drinkers quickly came to appreciate, including – perhaps especially – a thirst-quenching bitterness largely absent from ale. And the acids, as acids do, killed bacteria, so adding a third weapon to ale's antimicrobial armoury of alcohol and CO_2.

This antiseptic property was the game-changer. It has often been asserted that unhopped ale would sour in a few days. That's not necessarily true: an airtight cask of strong ale could survive the trip from London to Paris in good enough condition to impress a king, as we have seen. But the relatively short shelf-life of everyday English ale was undoubtedly a constraint on how a genuinely commercial brewery could grow. Extending the life of the product with an antibacterial agent such as the hop extended the range over which a brewery could trade and hence the volume that could viably be produced. The effectiveness of the hop was also such that the beer-brewer could make a weaker liquor, the hop acids taking over some of the protective duties of the alcohol. That meant less malt, and hence more profit, per brew. The downside was that the unfermented beer had to be boiled to get the best extract out of the hops (in contrast to the mashing of the malt, whose optimum extraction temperature is well below boiling point). Fuel for this additional process was expensive in the Middle Ages; but even that played into the hands of the big, well-capitalised urban brewer who could afford the additional expense and who, as time wore on, had more and more access to cheap coal. A further competitive advantage for beer was that hops, unlike the wide range of herbs that English alewives seem to have used, could be cultivated. No getting up early in the morning to go out gathering meadowsweet, bog myrtle, alehoof, yarrow, sweet gale or any of the other herbs that might go into ale: reliable supplies of dried hop cones, which would keep well enough until next year's harvest, simply arrived in enormous sacks or "pockets" from the hop-gardens of Kent and East Anglia, and that was that.

The first record of imported hopped beer, according to Cornell, was of a consignment from Holland which came into England through Great Yarmouth in 1361; the first record of hopped beer being imported to London comes only four years later. By this time hopped beer was already being widely traded over long distances throughout North-Western Europe and the first casks sent for sale in England were perhaps intended as a welcome taste of home for the many German, Dutch, Flemish and Scandinavian merchants based in the capital. But beer's appeal quickly spread beyond the community of homesick expats, and by the early 15th century at the latest it was routinely being brewed in England. An account from the reign of Henry V gives one reason for its popularity. The 200 tuns of ale ordered by the king to victual his army at the siege of Rouen in 1419 cost 30s apiece, while the 300 tuns of beer cost only 13s 4d. To survive the journey and to keep for a decent period once it had arrived, the ale had to be strong. That made it more than twice as expensive as the beer, which was why the king's victuallers ordered more beer than ale. It was this simple maths that drove beer brewing towards becoming a major industry and the part-time domestic ale-brewer gradually into extinction.

The story of hop cultivation in England is more complicated. Place-name evidence suggests that hops might have been grown in Worcestershire in Saxon times; but if so they were probably destined for use as a dyestuff rather than a flavouring for ale. Flemish weavers might have planted hop gardens in Kent in the early 14th century – again, probably as a dyestuff; and the Flemish connection is plainly to be seen by anyone driving through Kent today. The county is studded with drying sheds originally built for curing hops but now mostly converted into luxury houses. In Hereford and Worcester these are referred to simply as kilns; in Kent and Sussex they are oast-houses, from the Flemish or Dutch *eest*, meaning to dry. Hops, says Ian Hornsey, were recorded as being used for beer-brewing in Southwark from the 1420s; and from the evidence coming from the siege of Rouen, clearly beer-brewing was firmly established well before that, while at about the same time many other Flemish-derived brewing-related words – firkin, kilderkin, beer itself – were entering the language. The hops for Henry V's beer-order may well have come from these Kentish plantations, although they might equally have been imported. But it's hard to imagine a brewer paying for expensive imports if a cheaper locally-grown alternative were available, especially if price was part of his sales pitch.

For all its advantages, beer took a long time – three centuries or more – to drive unhopped ale out altogether and the process is not strictly part of our story. But it's interesting that ale-brewing hung on longest in the North of England, and that even after it had died out the usual Northern word for "beer" remained "ale". In the South-east "ale" more or less vanished as a word in everyday usage, surviving chiefly in brewery signage and advertising and also as a genteel euphemism. But when four beer-loving journalists got together in 1972 to start the backlash against keg, they called their organisation the Campaign for Real Ale, not beer. It was not an effort to be twee: all four were from Manchester.

CHAPTER 2: WINE, MEAD, AND CIDER

If ale was the drink of the common man – and, for everyday purposes, of the better-off as well – wine, mead, and cider were reserved to the tables of the wealthy and, perhaps on special occasions only, the aspiring. Wine was expensive because it was mostly imported; mead was expensive because honey was in such great demand as a culinary sweetener; and cider was expensive simply because it was so difficult to produce.

Wine

The Saxons were already familiar with wine when they embarked on their conquest of what was to become England, because by then they had already been in contact with Roman society for more than a century. As raiders, wine was part of their plunder. As mercenaries, it could have been part of their pay. As settlers, they would have found it in daily use among their Romanised neighbours. And after they rebelled in about 450 and started their conquest in earnest, they seem to have come across decaying memorials to Romano-British viticulture in the territories they captured, for there are notices of both neglected vineyards – *wilde wingearde* – and, in charters, to prominent *wintreows* or "wine-trees" as boundary markers, suggesting abandoned and overgrown grapevines. But there's no indication in these early days that the Saxon nobility gave up their ancestral mead in favour of wine, or that the Roman tradition of wine-making managed somehow to survive. For a revival in viticulture, we have to wait for the mission of St Augustine.

In the dog-eat-dog world of late 6th-century Anglo-Saxon politics, Kent sought the friendship and support of the powerful and sophisticated Frankish kingdom that lay just across the water. Kent was one of the smallest of the so-called heptarchy of English kingdoms that were fighting each other just as ferociously as they were completing their conquest of the Britons; and to strengthen his hand King Aethelbert first married a Christian Frankish princess and then in 597 agreed to convert his people to Christianity as well. With Christianity came the regular celebration of the Mass, and with the Mass came a continuous requirement for wine.

After his conversion, Aethelbert gave Augustine enough land to found a monastery. Within a few decades monasteries had spread across the whole of England as the engines of the conversion process: in 664 Whitby Abbey in faraway North Yorkshire hosted the Synod that united the Celtic and Saxon churches, and the Venerable Bede's monastery of Jarrow, 400 miles from Canterbury, was established by 680. Between Canterbury and Jarrow there lay many dozens of minsters and abbeys, some with only half-a-dozen brothers (and sisters – early Saxon monasteries usually had monks and nuns living cheek by jowl), some with more than a hundred. In the following two centuries viticulture became an established feature of monastic life. It is now argued that the creation of monastic vineyards was a commercial venture, rather than an attempt to secure the Church's supply of sacramental wine; for whatever reason, though, it is certain that monks planted vineyards As early as the 730s Bede recorded: "*On sumum stowum wingeardas growath*" – "in some places vineyards grow"; and by the later Saxon period viticulture appears to have been fairly widespread. In the mid-10th century King Eadwig gave a vineyard to Glastonbury Abbey; his successor Edgar gave one at Watchet to Abingdon Abbey *cum vinitoribus* – with vine-dressers; and in 990 a Bedfordshire widow named Aelfgifu left the produce of her vineyard to the Abbey of St Albans. Westminster Abbey owned vineyards at Staines. The produce of all these vineyards may well have been mostly or partly for sacramental use; but as a beverage, wine in later Saxon England was a high-status drink for the rich which might well have been a nice little earner, as Aelfric's late 10th-century *Colloquy* makes clear. "What do you drink?" asks the teacher. "*Ealu gif ic hæbbe, oppe wæter gif ic næbbe ealu* (ale if I have it, water if I don't)," replies the novice. "Don't you drink wine?" asks the teacher. "*Ic ne eom swa spedig þæt ic mæge bicgean me win; 7 wyn nis drenc cilda ne dysgra, ac ealdra 7 wisra* (I am not so rich that I can buy myself wine; and wine is not a drink for the young and foolish but for the old and wise)," is the reply.

For the Normans, by contrast, wine was the everyday drink for all but the poorest – and it wasn't the poorest who flocked to newly-conquered England in William's train, but the land-hungry younger sons of the gentry and ambitious mercenaries from adjoining regions: in short, people with a social standing to protect and enhance. The Conqueror's army of Norman, Breton, Flemish, and Northern French knights and their mesnies was at most 8,000 strong, maybe less. But his victory attracted still more soldiers as well as courtiers, clerics, merchants, and mere adventurers to exploit the new-won land, which they quickly set about transforming. London was given three castles – the Tower itself where the city wall meets the river in the east, Baynard's Castle at the western end of the wall, and Mountfichet's Castle to the north at Ludgate. They all had French garrisons. The Anglo-Saxon monks of Westminster and St Paul's were gradually squeezed out by French incomers. The new bourgeoisie, themselves French, endowed new monastic houses all peopled with Frenchmen. It's been estimated that around 20,000 Normans, plus their households, followed in the wake of the army, and they weren't confined to London. In Norwich, Anglo-Saxon townsmen were evicted both from the site of the new castle and from their old market, on which a Norman quarter was built. Other towns were also populated with politically reliable Franco-Norman burgesses and it is an entirely reasonable assumption that, as immigrants have always done, they brought with them their own customs and ways of life and tended to cleave together as a unit for both political and social reasons. (This was especially the case with foreign merchants, who were generally herded together by nationality in privileged ghettoes).

And they were wine-drinkers, these Normans. They are generally credited with introducing cider and cider-apples to Britain, but there is not a shred of documentary evidence for cidermaking in England until 1184, 30 years after the death of the last Norman king. Vineyards, however, had been planted in Normandy long before its conquest by Norse invaders: an 8th-century hagiography says of the region around Jumièges: "*hinc vinearum abundant butriones, qui turgentibus gemmis, lucentibus rutilant.*" (Here vineyards abound with bunches of grapes whose swelling buds gleam lustrously.") This was evidently good stuff, too: the writer uses the word *falernis*, Falernian, equating Norman wine, perhaps optimistically, with the very best Ancient Rome had to offer; and the uncouth Norse, who were granted the territory in 911, seem to have sought to emulate their more sophisticated Frankish neighbours by developing a taste for it. The annual fair at Rouen was one of North-western Europe's most important wine marts, where the vintages supplied to Aelfric's *ealdra 7 wisra* were almost certainly purchased. The Normans brought viticulture with them to England, too: 11 of the 38 vineyards listed in Domesday were new plantings. To a Norman in England, wine-drinking, even as it had been at the time of the *Colloquy*, was a sign of affluence and social standing – in short, of Norman-ness.

If the Normans were wine-drinkers, the Angevins who succeeded them when Henry II became king were even more so. Through his marriage to Eleanor of Aquitaine, Henry was already lord of the whole of south-western France with its established wine-producing regions in Anjou, along the Loire, around Bordeaux, and further south in Gascony. On his Coronation Day, 19th December 1154, his empire stretched from the Scottish marches to the Mediterranean. The French portion of the Angevin patrimony was a colossal producer and exporter of wine: by the beginning of the 14th century Gascony was exporting nearly 100,000 tuns (a tun being roughly a liquid ton or – even more roughly, given the vagaries of weights and measures at the time – 250 gallons) in a good year. The English portion was almost as prodigious an importer: it accounted for half of the output of Gascony, and yet more was sourced from other wine-producing regions including Germany, Spain, and those parts of the eastern Mediterranean still in Christian hands.

This was a time of rapid population growth, especially in towns and cities: London was home to about 20,000 people in 1100, 30,000 in 1200, and 80,000 in 1300. It was a time of increasing wealth, too; and meanwhile the ethnic, linguistic, and cultural divide between bourgeois conquerors and working-class conquered gradually healed with the passing generations. Down to the late 13th and early 14th centuries the nobility still spoke French, which was also the language of the law; increasingly, though, the burgeoning middle classes spoke and read English. But even though, like the bourgeoisie of all the great trading cities that fringed the North Sea, they regarded wine rather than ale as the drink most suited to their status, there was still something foreign and exotic about it: it came from across the sea, and the trade was under the control of merchants from across the sea.

There are records of English merchants carrying a certain amount of wine as part of a mixed cargo, but in the main the shipping was in the hands of Gascon or otherwise "foreign" merchants. For fear of pirates, most of the wine was transported in two great convoys whose arrival became quite an event. The first docked shortly after the *vendange*, when the new-made wine was still fermenting in its barrels; the other arrived in early summer when the wine had been matured for eight months or so. Some of the cargo was collected straight from the quay by major purchasers such as noble or ecclesiastical households; some was bought by native vintners directly off the ship; some went inland to the great fairs like those at Stourbridge Common at Cambridge in September and Wey Hill near Andover in October. But whoever their customers, the foreign shippers had only limited rights to travel and reside in England, and their cargoes therefore had to be sold quickly to English vintners for onward distribution.

This was an arrangement that underlined the truth that the English and Angevin halves of Henry II's empire never really became an integrated political unit, and attempts to knit it into one were fiercely resented. Edward I's *Carta Mercatoria* of 1303 exempted the foreign shippers from tolls, extended their residence permits, made special provision for the swift resolution of trade disputes, and allowed them to leave stock with "*privati*" or sales agents. These concessions, especially the last, were extremely unpopular with the "*indigeni*" or native vintners: when the shippers had to sell their wares straight off the boat they had to take whatever price they were offered, whereas *privati* could release stock on to the market at their own pace and hence at their own price. The *Carta Mercatoria* was one of the casualties of the frankly xenophobic rebellion of the Lords Ordainers against Edward II and his French "favourites" in 1311, and the exclusive right to wholesale wine and other imported goods around the country was restored to native traders.

Continuing conflict over control of the trade often saw foreign merchants becoming the targets of violent protest, but doesn't seem to have affected the middle class's preference for wine. For Chaucer, writing at the end of the 14th century, wine-drinking was a signifier of rank, or of aspiration or pretension to rank. Harry Bailey, the real-life host of the Tabard in Southwark where the 29 pilgrims of *Canterbury Tales* assembled for their journey, was a considerable figure in local politics. Chaucer assigns him the central role of shaping and directing the action of the poem, his authority underlined by the prestigious dinner he lays before his guests: "He served us with vitaille at the beste; strong was the wyn, and wel to drynke us leste". The Franklin also insists on the best, including a "sop in wyn" for breakfast; but his red face and his Epicurean belief that "pleyn delit/Was verray felicitee parfit" mark him out as a character of lower moral standing than the Host. As for the Summoner, as an officer of the ecclesiastical court he had benefit of clergy and therefore aspired to membership of the wine-drinking class; but morally, what a monster! Lecherous, corrupt, gluttonous, and cynical, "wel loved he garleek, onions, and eek lekes/And for to drynken strong wyn, reed as blood... He wolde suffer for a quart of wyn/A good fellawe to have his concubyn". So for Chaucer, wine-drinking might indicate social status, but social status was not necessarily equivalent to moral status.

Mead

Of apparently lower status than wine in later Saxon England, but very much the aristocrat of drinks in the 8th-century saga *Beowulf*, was mead. If wine was the preferred drink of the old and wise, mead was the drink of heroes. And not just to the Saxons, either, but to the doomed British warriors of *Y Goddodin*, which is roughly contemporary with *Beowulf*. Even in the very last years of the 10th century, more than a century after Aelfric's *Colloquy* and at a time when the upper echelons of English society were already becoming Normanised, a heroic saga was not complete without its reference to mead. *"Gemunað þara mæla þe we oft æt meodo spræcan/þonne we on benc beot ahofon, hælað on healle"* – "remember the words we spoke so often over the mead, when we heroes boasted on the benches in the hall", laments Aelfwine in *The Battle of Maldon,* composed shortly after the battle which was fought in 991. In reality Byrhtnoth, earl of East Anglia and the hero of the poem, probably drank as much wine as mead.

Judging by the Sanskrit derivation of its name, and given the simplicity of its manufacture (honey mixed with water in the ratio of 1:4 or thereabouts, boiled, skimmed, and left to be fermented by wild yeasts), mead is likely to be one of mankind's oldest alcoholic beverages. But the fact that it's made by the simplest process, along with palm and sap wines, in the entire alcoholic gamut doesn't make it easy to get. Honey has been prized for its sweetness for millennia, but wild bees don't surrender it without a fight. They build their hives in inaccessible places and are quite capable of defending them against scavengers. Nevertheless, so prized is honey among peoples with little or no access to other sources of sugar that even today tribespeople in the remote forests of Papua New Guinea and elsewhere will cheerfully risk life and limb to get it.

Apiculture appears to have been developed in about 2500BC by that most inventive of societies, the Ancient Egyptians, spreading in succeeding centuries throughout the eastern Mediterranean. Given honey's importance, apiculture became a highly-organised industry: an archaeological site in the Jordan Valley has yielded 30 intact hives made of clay and straw in a complex that could have accommodated 100 such hives, yielding 1,000lbs of honey and 200lbs of wax a year. It dates to around 900BC. Roman writers talked extensively about beekeeping in works ranging from poetry (Virgil's *Georgics*) to estate management (Columella's *De Re Rustica*). And although wine was the chief beverage of Rome, the Romans made mead as well: Columella gives a basic recipe, but there were other honey-based or honey-flavoured drinks too. *Hydromellum* (*milititis* to Pliny the Elder) was basic mead made with four parts water to one part honey; *mulsum* was grape wine sweetened with honey.

Beekeeping appears to have been one of the arts of antiquity not known to the first Saxon invaders, who collected wild honey from the hills (*dunhunige*) and fields (*feldbeon hunig*). Honey was therefore a luxury, and mead an extremely expensive tipple. But, as with winegrowing, the spread of Christianity ensured that beekeeping became an important part of agriculture, since beeswax was required for church candles at least on important occasions (tallow sufficed for everyday use, even in church). By the early 11th century the handbook of estate management, *Rectitudines Singularum Personum*, could list the *beoceorl* or beekeeper among the normal personnel of a landed estate; and although the *beoceorl* was in the lowest rank of free men alongside the swineherd, the value of the honey he harvested can be judged from the size of the measure by which it was commonly assessed for the purpose of rents and taxes. Ale was measured by the *amber*, which was almost as large as a modern brewer's barrel of 36 gallons; honey, however, was measured by the *sester*, which at that time was about equivalent to a pint. Honey-rents recorded in Domesday were paid in small quantities: the tax paid by the manor of Oxford, for instance, included a mere six sesters of honey. Seen in this light, the fine of a sester of honey levied on members of the Cambridge Thegn's Guild for non-attendance at official functions was not a negligible one.

Mead almost disappeared from the written record after the Conquest. This is hardly surprising: the new rulers were wine-drinking Frenchmen – as indeed, to an extent, was the last Saxon king (but one), Edward the Confessor. At his accession in 1042 at the age of 39 he had lived in exile in Normandy for 26 years. His mother was a Norman – Ethelred the Unready's second wife Emma, Duke Richard of Normandy's sister – and he did his best, although without much success, to staff his government with his Norman cousins and in-laws. Ralph, the Norman Earl of Hereford, proved no match for Welsh insurgents, while Eustace of Boulogne was so harsh and high-handed that he provoked riots in Dover which very nearly led to civil war. Robert of Jumièges, Edward's Archbishop of Canterbury, soon fell out with the English aristocracy and was deposed and exiled after only 18 months in office. Nevertheless, these were Edward's chosen associates, and not one of them spoke English. (Edward himself may not have spoken English particularly well). Not one of them habitually drank mead, either. After the Conquest the Normanisation of the upper echelons of society was swift, and mead was eclipsed at the high tables by wine.

That doesn't mean that it died out, though. Honey and beeswax were still both vital commodities and still in regular production, and although honey's principal role was as the cook's only readily-available sweetener there was still a supply for fermentation purposes. Beekeepers had not yet learnt to separate the honey from the combs by centrifugal force and instead, after collecting the free-running honey, smashed up the combs to make wax. The combs had to be thoroughly rinsed to clean them of any remaining honey, and the sweet rinsing water was a ready-made must that could only be turned into mead or tipped away. But this can only have been a small-scale rustic operation, a by-product of manorial beekeeping, and certainly nothing that could compete in the market against the virtual mass-production and highly organised distribution of vast quantities of Gascon and other imported wines; so mead was both economically and culturally marginalised.

Nonetheless, production continued, and the honey-must was often blended with other fermentables or aromatics to provide a number of hybrids, some of which were highly prized. Honey-must fermented with grape juice and spices, for instance, made piment (also sometimes and inaccurately called hippocras, which was strictly speaking a spiced white wine). Given the high price of spices and the laborious method of filtration through bags of aromatics by which piment was made it must have been expensive, and was definitely an aristocratic pleasure. There's a recipe for piment (wrongly given as ypocras) in *The Forme of Cury*, England's first cook-book, published in 1390, that includes ginger, spikenard, galingale, cloves, gillyflower, long pepper, nutmeg, marjoram, and grains of paradise. The authors of the book were Richard II's personal cooks, so we can be sure that piment was served at the royal table. A pipe of it – that's about 100 gallons – was among the wines served at the enthronement of George Neville as Archbishop of York in 1465. Interestingly, piment was habitually served in later years as an aperitif, which suggests that it was dry. We often think of mead as a sweet drink because of the association with honey; but of course the sugars in honey, as in any other base, can be fermented out to complete or near-complete dryness. Perhaps piment was something like dry vermouth. A close cousin was metheglyn from the Welsh *meddyg* + *glyn*, literally "healing drink". This was mead in which curative herbs had been macerated and was often taken as a digestif.

Particularly useful on the manor was melomel, honey-must fermented with fruit juice (unless the fruit used was mulberries, in which case it was called morat or murrey). In medieval times, centuries before cheap, industrially-refined beet sugar became available, fruit-growers couldn't turn their surpluses into jam, as they did from the early 19th century on. (Several of the best-known names in jam-making today, including Chivers and Wilkins, started their corporate lives as soft-fruit growers and only began making conserves as a way of squeezing a profit out of their surpluses and discards). Nor could they make straightforward fruit wines, since even modern strains of soft fruit aren't sweet enough to ferment without added sugar. In a "hit" year, therefore, the only thing to do with all those leftover plums, gages, blackberries, strawberries, blackcurrants, redcurrants and so on was to pulp them and add them to the honey-must. Melomel therefore provided the steward of a knightly or monastic estate with a way of turning a profit on produce that would otherwise have had to be left to rot – which, given the care with which landowners scrutinised their stewards' and bailiffs' accounts, must have been very welcome.

When wine was king, then, mead and its variants seem to have occupied the position of modern-day liqueurs: secondary in terms of volume and profile, maybe, but drinks for which there still was a strong demand – and demand at the sophisticated end of the spectrum, at that. To return to Chaucer, and the *Miller's Tale*, when the insufferable Absolon (he who was on the receiving end of the most famous fart in literature) is trying to impress the fair Abigail (whose mouth was "as sweete as bragot or the meeth"), "he sent her piment, meeth, and spiced ale/And wafres, piping hot..." and again, "for she was of the town, he profred meed". Note that, for all that mead can be as sweet or as dry as the maker requires, to Chaucer it was a sweet drink favoured by sophisticated young women "of the town". The Bailey's of its day, perhaps?

Cider

Eyebrows will doubtless be raised by my lumping cider in with wine and mead as a preserve of the middle and upper classes: it certainly doesn't have that cachet today. But of all the sources of fermentable material available in medieval times apples were the hardest to process, needing heavy-duty equipment to crack – expensive equipment, available only to those with capital. Honey requires no kit at all to separate it from its sugar: it *is* sugar. Grapes want nothing more complicated than a trough and a few willing pairs of feet. Even malt can be coarsely ground with a hand-quern to yield enough grist for a single mash. But apples have fantastic compressive strength. Step on one and you'll squash it: step on two or three and they'll bear your weight. Imagine, then, the pressure you have to be able to apply to crush a worthwhile quantity. So if you want to get at the juice you need not just one piece of heavy equipment but two: a mill to grind the fruit, and a press to extract the juice from the pulp.

The grinding would be no problem: given a good strong tub, a chunky enough baton of wood, a spare afternoon, and plenty of energy and you can crush enough apples to be worth pressing. The trough-mill, the standard apparatus for crushing apples in any quantity right up to the mid-20th century, is more sophisticated but still a fairly simple piece of kit derived ultimately from the olive-crusher of Classical Antiquity still reputedly in use in remoter parts of Greece today. It's no more than a circular trough with a millstone standing upright in it; the millstone has an axle running through it which is attached to a rotating central pillar at one end and a horse (or, in the case of the ancient olive-crusher, a slave) at the other. Pour the fruit into the trough, gee up the horse (or the slave), and there you have it: press-ready pulp. You can even get away with using a second-quality millstone which would shatter explosively if rotated at the speed it would reach in a water- or windmill, but wouldn't if it were turned at the more sedate pace of a bored horse (or slave).

It still takes incredible pressure to squeeze the juice out of the pulp, though: some small-scale producers today use an upside-down lorry-jack which can lift several tons. For the ancients it was a big problem, but one they were eager to solve. A ton of apples should yield more than 150 gallons of fermentable juice, as well as 250-300lbs of squeezed-out pulp to feed to the animals – so, quite a valuable crop. In Republican Rome landowners with the money to invest could build the kind of giant beam press described by Cato in the 2nd century BC, which was a fearsomely efficient extractor of juice but very unwieldy. Still, landowners were evidently willing to make the investment: two centuries later Pliny the Elder wrote casually that what he called "artificial" wine was made of pears and all kinds of apples – the first written record of cidermaking in history.

By Pliny's time, though, the pressing problem had been solved. His contemporary, Hero of Alexandria, described in his *Mechanica* a new device that could achieve the necessary pressure for a fraction of the investment demanded by the lever-press: the screw-press. This simple machine was one of the technological triumphs of the ancient world, making possible the mass production of all kinds of goods that we take for granted: paper, printed fabrics, pasteboard, nut and seed oils – and cider. Its use spread rapidly throughout the Roman world and it remained the foundation of a host of industries for almost two millennia. Its one drawback was that before the invention of the thread-cutting lathe in the late 18th century the corresponding threads had to be crafted by hand and eye, which required both skill and time and therefore made the apparatus and its products expensive. Many of the goods made on screw-presses were therefore luxuries in medieval times: pasteboard playing cards are one example; and with nut and seed oils at a premium, oil-lamps had to wait until the rise of commercial whaling to replace tallow candles in everyday use.

But the screw-press could also have the opposite effect, making cheap what had previously been expensive. For instance, William Caxton set up the first printing press in England in 1476, which made printed books much, much cheaper and more accessible than their hand-copied predecessors. You might even say that the screw-press gave us Shakespeare. It doesn't seem to have given us cider, though – or not in early medieval times, at least. For there is no evidence that the Saxons, who came from outside the boundaries of the Roman Empire, ever used or even knew of the screw-press. And if they had no screw-press, they had no cider.

In *Golden Fire: The Story of Cider* (Bright Pen Books, 2012) I argued at some length against the recent identification of a strong, sweet liquor called *beor* by the Saxons with cider. *Beor* had generally been taken as just another word for ale until Ann Hagen (*Anglo-Saxon Food & Drink*, Anglo-Saxon Books 2006) made a vigorous case for it as cider. Her argument is many-pronged. First, she says, *beor* is not cognate with beer but comes from an Old Norse word, *bjorr*, meaning strong drink. Second, it is sometimes associated in the texts where it is mentioned with expressions such as *ofetes wos* (fruit juice) and *gewrungen* (squeezed or pressed). Third, it is always described as a high-value drink, very much stronger, sweeter, and more expensive than ale.

But although Hagen herself has collected some 50 Old English wine compound words of which 35 relate to vine growing and wine production – *wincole*, *winseax*, *winbeam* – she has found no compound suggesting awareness of the mechanical press the cidermaker needs. The Continental peoples the Saxons traded with made so much wine that they surely used screw-presses; and since there are scattered references to cider in early medieval Breton and Frankish literature – in Charlemagne's capitulary *De Villis* of c800AD cider and perry are called *pomatium* and *pyratium* respectively – we can conclude that they definitely did. But the technology never seems to have crossed the Channel.

And there's another problem. The word *beor* almost always occurs in contexts implying both sweetness and strength which with cider, you can't have. In a hot, dry, growing season apple juice will contain enough sugar to yield a cider of about 8.5% ABV; 6.5-7.5% is more usual. So cider is at best only as strong as the most alcoholic of beers, and at that strength it cannot be sweet. Cider yeasts are voracious and fruit sugars are easily digestible, so a strong cider will ferment out to near-complete dryness. Sweet ciders are generally very low in alcohol because they are made by deliberately inhibiting fermentation: modern French examples are often below 3%.

The simplest method of making a drink that was both strong and sweet using the technology available at the time was to brew ale using a much higher ratio of malt to water. The yeast will be poisoned by its own alcohol and CO_2 before all the malt sugars have been converted into alcohol, yielding ale of 7%-9% alcohol by volume with plenty of residual sweetness. And indeed altering the malt-to-water ratio has been the standard method of varying the strength of ale since brewing began; but strong ale or beer is expensive to make because of the amount of malt required, and was therefore the preserve of the better-off. Nor need the identification of *beor* with fruit juice detain us: we know that Saxon meadmakers dosed their products with honey, spices, and mulberries, while Saxon brewers also added honey and spices to their ale. It seems rather like straining on a gnat to baulk at the possibility that *beor* might simply have been dosed with *ofetes wos*, just as some Belgian ales are today.

But if the Saxons didn't give us cider, who did? The traditional culprits are the Normans, but there is no evidence to support the idea. In the century after the Conquest there is no record of cider, and in a search of the National Archives the community archaeologist Rebecca Roseff (www.historyatthecidermuseum.org.uk/orchards) found just 11 unequivocal records between the years 1200 and 1475. The earliest, from 1200, mentions a *pressurhus* with outbuildings including a cider mill (*molendina ad poma*) in Staffordshire. Another of Roseff's records – from Sussex in 1349 – is especially useful because it gives us a price: £34 6s 8d for 52½ barrels.

The first of these records comes not from the Norman era but from the Plantagenet. And indeed the earliest unequivocal record of cider in England is also Plantagenet, predating the Staffordshire "*pressurhus*" by only 16 years. It comes in the pipe roll – the record of royal income and expenditure – for 1184. William FitzRobert, Earl of Gloucester, had died without an heir the previous year, and among the revenues of his vacant estates accruing to the king were the proceeds of sales of meat, grain, wool, cheese, wine... and cider.

As we have seen, Henry II, the first Plantagenet, succeeded the last of the Normans in 1154 and brought with him as a dowry the enormous Angevin lands of South-West France, notably Bordeaux and Gascony. These were already important wine-producing regions, and a big trade soon sprang up between La Rochelle and London. Perhaps the trade was not only in wine, but also in the technology used for making it on a near-industrial scale – notably the screw press that the Saxons lacked. A charter of 1230 granting Bishop Jocelyn of Bath the lease of a cider press hints that this may be so; and the written evidence seems to reinforce the idea that widespread cidermaking was not after all introduced by the Normans but by the Plantagenets more than a century later.

There are, of course, many more medieval references to cider than are contained in the National Archive. In Norfolk in 1204, Robert de Evermere of Runham paid a quantity of pearmains and four tuns (*modios*) of the wine made from them annually as rent. Then there's the most memorable of them all from 12 years later, Roger of Wendover's euphemistic attribution of the death of King John in 1216 to a surfeit of "peaches and new cider". The economic historian Louis Francis Salzman records in *Industries of the Middle Ages* (1913), the 12th-century writer Gerald de Barri's characterisation of its consumption by the monks of Canterbury instead of ale as an instance of their luxury. In 1212 the sale of cider was a source of income for Battle Abbey, some of it coming from the monastery's estate at Wye, Kent, which was still producing a good deal of cider during the 14th century. Cider was imported from Normandy to Winchelsea in 1270, while at Pagham a mill and press were wrongfully seized by the escheator's officer in 1275, and at the same place in 1313 the archbishop's bailiff had to account for 12 shillings spent on buying four cider casks, repairing a press, and hiring men to make the cider. In the county rolls of 1341 no fewer than 80 parishes in West Sussex were reported as paying their tithes in cider, amounting to £5 in Easebourne and 10 marks (£6 13s 4d) at Wisborough where in 1385 William Threle granted gardens and orchards to John Pakenham, reserving to himself the produce of half the trees whether for eating or for cider (*mangable et ciserable*) at an annual rent of a pipe of cider and a quarter of store apples (*hordapplen*); he also retained the right to use the "wringehouse" and its press for his fruit. Peter Clark cites research showing that the manor of Alciston in Sussex produced some 500 gallons a year throughout the later Middle Ages and says that the manorial orchards at Banham, Norfolk, yielded enough apples in 1281 to make three casks of cider worth 10 shillings each. And Alicia Amherst's *History of Gardening in England*, published in 1895, quotes the bailiff's accounts for the Earl of Devon's Exminster manor listing cidermaking as a regular source of revenue in 1285-6; while at Plympton in the same year a small surplus is recorded as remaining from the previous season. The Almoner of Winchester Abbey, however, mournfully records in his accounts for 1352: "*et de cisera nihil, quia non fuerunt poma hoc anno*" – "and of cider none, because there were no apples this year". And well might he have been mournful, for cider sales could be a good source of income: in 1388, for instance, the garden accounts of Abingdon Abbey include 13s 4d "*de cicera vendita*".

The one thing that all these references have in common is that they characterise cidermaking as a seigneurial activity rather than a peasant one. The necessary equipment and labour (and apple-picking is a labour-intensive affair) might have been within the resources of the lord of a reasonably prosperous manor, but only if it was a paying proposition. And it could be: cider fetched 2½d-4d a gallon, as reckoned by Roseff on the basis of the Shoreham figures, compared to ¾d-1½d a gallon for ale. At that price, cider can only have been a drink for the middle and upper classes.

CHAPTER 3: THE OLDE ENGLISH ALEHOUSE

Because Medieval England was overwhelmingly rural, it seems to make sense to look for the origins of the pub in the countryside where the vast majority of potential customers lived. And after all, the English pub is an essential component of the archetypal English village. Without a pub, a village is no more than a collection of houses. The fact that so many villages have been left without pubs in the long stream of closures since the 1960s is cited as a major cause of the decline of the communal spirit of the village, although it might equally be argued that it is the result rather than the cause. Nevertheless, a village without a pub is somehow less of a village than a village with one. So central to the common mind-picture of an English village is a cosy pub, so unalterable and immemorial does it seem, that it comes as something of a surprise to discover how shallow the historical roots of the village pub really are.

So fixed, indeed, is this idea of the pub as the indispensable heart of village society that many writers have tried to trace its history back to Saxon England and further, to the Roman occupation. And indeed we do know that throughout the Roman Empire there were both urban taverns and country inns. Frederick Hackwood in *Inns, Ales and Drinking Customs of Old England* (1909) – a *tour de force* of Edwardian antiquarianism that has become a classic since it was reprinted a few years ago – explains how Roman roads were regularly punctuated by *mansiones*, or government hostels for travellers on official business, with *mutationes* or posting-stations at convenient intervals in between. Then there were also the urban *thermopolia*, which you can see for yourself in Pompeii and Herculaneum and which Hackwood describes as "the prototype of the good old English hostelry" (although if he'd known more about what went on in some *thermopolia* he might have revised his judgement).

Given the complete disruption of society in Britain in the fifth and sixth centuries, however, it is impossible to trace any kind of continuity between Pompeian *thermopolia* and the hostelries of Medieval England, and perhaps even ridiculous to try. It is also hard to see how anything like the elaborate system of *mutationes* and *mansiones* could have survived either, as they were part of an economy and a system of government that disappeared utterly. For what has only recently been shown is the rapid and almost total desertion of Britain's cities once their political and economic ties with the Continent were severed early in the fifth century. The one thing cities need is money, and with no taxes and no trade to sustain it urban life in post-Roman Britain starved to death with surprising speed. Canterbury seems to have survived in some form since it was closest to the source of the Anglo-Saxon irruption and became the seat of the local monarchy; but archaeologists have found nothing but a few scraps of broken pottery from late fifth century York, Chester, and Gloucester; and while an army of defeated Britons was still able to take shelter behind London's Roman walls after the battle of Crayford in 457, they probably found nothing within but ruins. How the power-vacuum caused by the collapse of the urban economy with its market for agricultural produce was filled can only be conjectured. In the more rugged uplands of the North and West we can actually trace kingdoms coalescing around local leaders who were perhaps not entirely Romanised; in the more thoroughly civilised South and East it is harder to see the villa-dwelling landed proprietors making much of an army out of their virtually enslaved workforces. And indeed once the Saxon revolt had started the South-east succumbed quite quickly, leaving nothing of Roman forms and culture and, as far as we can tell, no more than a remnant population of subjugated British peasants among whom even Christianity may quickly have died out.

The Anglo-Saxon Mead Hall

So Southern and Eastern England were effectively a *tabula rasa* for the settlers who followed the conquerors. Even British place-names vanished, with the exception of the river-names which the Saxons will have discovered when using navigable waterways as military roads. The economic and social structure of the villages they founded was, therefore, entirely their own. Here, the basic unit was the kindred group or *maeg-burg*, and the focus of society was the meadhall where food and drink were freely dispensed to the royal or noble family and its followers and guests. Anglo-Saxon literature is replete with references to and tales of warriors feasting and quarrelling in their meadhalls – *Heorot*, the meadhall of King Hrothgar, provides the central image of the *Beowulf* saga as a near-sacred place that contains and defines the whole spirit of the people.

Intriguingly, modern archaeology suggests that a hall – although not, perhaps, quite as grand as *Heorot* – played a similar role in the lives of ordinary people. West Stow, an early Anglian settlement well-preserved by the sandy soil of the Thetford Forest in Norfolk, appears to have been laid out as an aggregation of around half-a-dozen compounds or hut groups, each comprising one comparatively large building surrounded by five or six smaller ones. It is assumed that each hut group pertained to a single kindred whose members either bunked in the larger building and worked in the smaller ones, or slept in the smaller and messed in the larger. Whichever alternative is true (and the Venerable Bede, below, strongly suggests the latter), in either case the kindred seems to have shared the larger building and to have eaten and drank there communally making it, albeit on socially much humbler terms, their equivalent of the royal or noble meadhall.

West Stow was abandoned at some time between 720 and 750AD, just when Bede was writing his *Historia Ecclesiastica Gentis Anglorum* which perhaps gives us a sly glimpse of what went on in its kindred-group halls. Here Bede describes how Caedmon, a humble swineherd at Whitby Abbey 50 years previously who became famous as a devotional poet, was originally too shy to sing in public:

"He wæs gelyfdre ylde, 7 næfre nænig leoð geleornade. Ond he forþon oft in gebeorscipe, þonne þær wæs blisse intinga gedemed, þæt heo ealle sceolden þhur endebyrdnesse be hearpan singan, þonne he geseah þa hearpen nealecan, þonne aras he for scome from þæm symble 7 ham eode to his huse." (He was quite old and had never learnt any songs. For that reason, often at a party when a theme for the festivities had been decided on and the harp was passed round for everyone to contribute a song, he would see his turn coming and, out of embarrassment, would get up from the feast and go to his house). It should be noted that Caedmon leaves the common gathering to return to his own sleeping-place. But what else can this extract tell us?

Obviously these *beorscipe* were fairly formal events – the passage even uses the world *symble*, normally reserved for official diplomatic feasts, rather like a modern state banquet, at which there were speeches, music, and gift-giving. The karaoke nights that Caedmon fled in embarrassment were clearly less elevated than that, but Bede's description implies that leisure in his time was not an entirely casual affair. It's a shame that Anglo-Saxon writers didn't consider the daily life of the peasantry a worthy subject for closer attention; but among the 2,000 or so surviving texts are numerous religious canons or law-codes attempting to forbid priests from attending *beorscipe* and showing off their talents as singers and story-tellers; and it should be noted that the parties at which Caedmon was an unwilling guest were thrown by the monks who employed him. The songs he was ashamed not to know were therefore religious in character rather than the bawdier verses they might have been singing in the kindred halls of West Stow.

Another important point that emerges here is that while we know quite a lot from a variety of sources about what the Anglo-Saxons drank and when and where they drank it, we very rarely hear of ale being bought and sold. That doesn't mean it was never bought and sold: the Domesday Book entry for Chester records that in the days of Edward the Confessor brewers who used short measure could be fine four shillings; if they brewed bad ale they could either be fined or ducked. But Chester was, by the standard of the times, a veritable metropolis with 431 taxable households, another 56 belonging to the bishop, and who knows how many too poor to be taxed. In the countryside, given the communal lifestyle of the kindred and its hall, it's fair to assume that brewing was not the commercial enterprise it became in the 12th and 13th centuries and that ale was put on the table for all comers just like the bread, cheese, and pickle of an old-fashioned farm kitchen. It had a value, for rents and taxes might in some cases be paid in it; but this kind of equivalence – a tribute in kind raised from the whole community, or from an estate – is not the same thing as a monetary price. And even if there was trade of a sort in ale, the one thing we can say is that it wasn't an organised, formal, truly commercial trade. We're certainly not looking at anything like a pub.

And then, in the 10th century, come two sticks of legislative dynamite that raise the intriguing possibility that someone, somewhere, in later Anglo-Saxon England had the idea of throwing open their doors to drinkers – of inventing the pub, in fact.

The first of these thin splinters of evidence comes from the 18th-century antiquarian Joseph Strutt who, in *Horda: A Complete View of the Manners, Customs, etc of the Inhabitants of England* (1774), states that King Edgar (959-75), "by the advice of (St) Dunstan, put down many alehouses, suffering only one to be in a village or small town". Strutt offers no documentary support for this other than an unidentifiable attribution to William of Malmesbury, nor a Latin or Old English original for the word he translates as "alehouse"; and without that it's impossible to make sense of it. On the face of it, therefore, it still seems unlikely that there was any such thing as an alehouse in the mid-10th century, nor anything that would come close to the description, at the time. Perhaps, if the legislation exists at all, it was aimed at consolidating the many kindred halls into one single village focus, a subject we shall return to.

The second piece of evidence is rather more interesting but scarcely more helpful. A decree issued by Ethelred the Unready in the closing years of the 10th century fixes the fine for public brawling thus: *"And if man sylle on æla huse, þete man þæt æt deadum mann mid vi healfmarce 7 æt cwicon mid xii oran."* (And if anyone brawls in an alehouse so that someone is killed he shall pay six half-marks; or if no-one is killed, 12 *ore*). So: an apparently unequivocal reference to the alehouse; but (as far as I can tell) completely solitary and, thanks to the near-death of written English after the Conquest, not to be repeated for many generations. Does *"eala huse"* simply mean kindred hall? It seems to be the likeliest option.

A third contemporary reference to a *hus* where ale was available doesn't offer us much help either. In the 990s Aelfric – he of the *Colloquy* – produced a set of sermons for saints' days. In the sermon regarding the martyrdom of King Oswald of Northumbria in 642, he recounts how a horseman set out for home from the battlefield at Oswestry where the king had been killed by his pagan enemies: *"Þa gemette he gebeoras bliðe æt þam huse ... 7 sæt mid þam gebeorum blissigende samod. Man wohrte þa micel fyr tomiddes ðam gebeorum 7 þa spearcan wundom wið þæs rofes swyðe oð þæt hus færlice eall on fyre wearð..."* (Then he met happy beer-drinkers at a house ... and sat with them making merry together. Someone lit a great fire in the middle of the drinkers; the sparks went swiftly up to the roof, and suddenly the house was all ablaze...)

The horseman doesn't seem to have been much affected by the death of his king; but the story doesn't get us much further forward in our hunt for an Anglo-Saxon pub. All we discover is that a traveller could expect to join in wherever ale and good company presented themselves; we don't discover whether the ale and good company were available at a permanent commercial establishment or in a kindred hall, or even whether the traveller was expected to pay. The confident assertion (which first surfaced, as far as I can tell, as a completely unsupported assertion in 1825 in Thomas Fosbroke's *Encyclopeadia of Antiquities* and has been unquestioningly followed by succeeding generations of writers) that there were three kinds of drinking establishment open to the public of Saxon England, the *eala-hus* or alehouse, the *win-hus* or tavern, and the *cumen-hus* or inn therefore seems unfounded.

Churches as Social Centres

Whether the kindred hall survived the Conquest in some form, or whether the new Norman and Northern French manorial lords rapidly suppressed establishments where subjugated peasants might meet to talk sedition in a language their new masters couldn't understand, is unknowable, but it seems unlikely. For towards the end of the Saxon period, and more rapidly so after the Conquest, English villages were acquiring new focuses of communal life to usurp the hall's social function: the village church.

One of the many reasons why there are so few surviving pre-Conquest village churches around is that there wasn't a huge number of them in the first place. Immediately after 597 the campaign of converting the country was conducted from great monastic missionary centres, many of them founded in or near seats of royal power. These monasteries established smaller daughter-houses – collegiate, like their parent monasteries, and known as "minsters" – in regional centres, from which priests made circuits of the districts in their care, often saying Mass and preaching at stone crosses put up for the purpose. In time local magnates began to build small churches on their estates, partly out of piety, partly as a mark of ownership; but these were privately owned and maintained, and Saxon England knew nothing like the parish system that slowly evolved after the Conquest. By the time of the Conquest, however, the tradition of founding private chapels and churches was already well-established, and it was continued by the new aristocracy who were, understandably, even more keen to mark their territory than the Anglo-Saxon lords they had ejected. By the late 13th century England had around 8,000 parishes subject to Papal taxation, a tally that remained largely unaltered until the Industrial Revolution.

If the law cited by Strutt restricting villages to one "alehouse" each actually existed, perhaps it related to this expansion in the number of local churches. Perhaps King Edgar and his spiritual mentor St Dunstan saw an opportunity to abolish the old ancestral institution, the kindred hall, where feuds between families might be nurtured and intracommunal violence stirred up, and replace it with a single communal focus that was as much spiritual as social and was under the guidance of a resident full-time priest. It would certainly fit with Dunstan's programme of moral reform; but without a text we will never know. Nonetheless, local churches did rapidly assume the role of the modern village hall or functions suite where religious and non-religious festivities were commonly staged; and they retained it throughout the Middle Ages and well into the modern period.

When local churches hosted scot-ales, bid-ales, bride-ales, help-ales and all the other variants of the rent party or charity fundraiser that were current, the necessary malt was requisitioned by the churchwardens, brewed under their supervision, and then sold back to the people who had supplied it in the first place. It was one thing for kin groups to brew, effectively, for the family dining table; quite another to brew for the whole village. That would feel like work, which had a value – and now, for the very first time, the local authorities were putting a monetary price on it. For it cannot be coincidental, but only when village life begins to crystallise around one innovation – the local church – do we find another: brewing for sale. At the same time as largely or partly self-sufficient extended kin groups were losing their separate identities, then, what had once been provided free within the family was becoming an item of exchange.

Ale for Sale

It's easy to imagine how this process might have got under way. In an extended family sharing a communal kitchen, there would almost always be somebody available to cook the pottage – and brew the ale – whatever the exigency of the moment. But in a single-family household, the cook/brewer's indisposition through illness or childbirth might mean the rest of the family going without. A friend or relation might be able to step in; but if not, the options were either to borrow or to barter... and borrowing and barter are but a short step from buying. By the middle of the 12th century at least, and probably even earlier, there was a lively trade in ale in villages up and down the country.

Any innovation in a society that placed such great weight on custom and tradition was bound to attract the attention of the authorities. We have already seen that in late Anglo-Saxon Chester – an important port with, no doubt, a disproportionate number of transients among its population – ale was brewed for retail and its price and measure were regulated, with fines or worse imposed on transgressors. One of William the Conqueror's earliest enactments, a decree of 1068, regulated weights and measures while making it clear that the new king was following sound Anglo-Saxon precedent – "*Et quod habeant per universum regnum, mensuras fidelissimas et signatas, et pondera fidelissima et signata, sicut boni praedecessores statuerunt.*" (They shall keep throughout the realm most faithful and marked measures and most faithful and marked weights, as our worthy predecessors have decreed) – and although the decree does not specifically mention ale, it was clearly covered by the legislation. From incomplete records it seems that newly-chartered boroughs were the first to assume the right to control the price, quality, and measure of ale brewed for sale (and bread, too, which was also becoming a trading commodity for much the same reasons). In the countryside some landlords, seeing a commercial activity they could tax, simply charged a fee, generally called alesilver or "tolcester" (from "toll" and "sester" or measure) for the right to brew for sale. The overwhelming majority of manors, though, adopted the same practice – called an "assize" or assessment – as the boroughs.

The assize is commonly portrayed as little more than a cash-grab by exploitative landlords; and in time it may have become so, with fines for the generally unspecified offence of "brewing outside the assize" representing a significant proportion of the lord's customary profits of justice. But it may be a little harsh to assume that things were ever thus, and that the assize was never anything more than yet another of the many manifestations of official extortion under which the medieval working class laboured. First, it has to be remembered that not all law was imposed from above. In chartered boroughs the burgesses themselves fought for and often won the right to make their own regulations, while on rural manors it was generally the jurors of the manorial court – effectively, the village elders – who agreed what was "customary" and therefore permissible and what was not. And the assize, unlike seigneurial impositions such as the heriot, did confer a general benefit: nobody, after all, likes to be overcharged for a short measure of weak, oxidised ale. Second, the first attempt at a national codification of the assize came in the second half of the reign of Richard I, the absentee king. The four justiciars he appointed to manage the country while he was off warmongering were all salaried civil servants who had worked their way up from being clerks of chancery. They were not landowners with a personal stake in overtaxing the peasantry; rather, they were professional bureaucrats whose prime concern was to support and enhance the Plan-tagenet monarchy through sound organisation and effective regulation. Indeed, standard weights and measures were considered so important that they were included in the Magna Carta of 1215: "*Una mensura vini sit per totum regnum nostrum & una mensura cervise.*" (Let there be one measure of wine throughout our realm, and one measure of ale). Third, the assize is always taken to be a thinly-veiled revenue raiser because so many brewsters were presented and fined for breaching it – a third of all the female inhabitants in the manors studied by Judith M Bennett. But what we can't say, of course, is whether the other two-thirds also brewed for sale from time to time but don't appear in the records because they observed the assize. If that is indeed the case then there might have considerable resentment of those brewsters who were frequent offenders; and the cheating alewife is a stock figure in medieval satire of various kinds from ballads to church carvings.

The Assize of Bread and Ale was fully stated as a national statute, complete with detailed tariff, for the first time in 1267, and was slightly but, for the purposes of this study, very significantly amended a decade later. It tied the permitted retail price of ale to the fluctuating price of grain: in normal times, urban brewers were allowed to charge 1½d a gallon; in the country, where overheads were presumably lower, they were allowed to charge only a penny. The ale could only be sold in containers of a quart, a pottle (half-gallon), or a gallon, which had to be tested and stamped by the manor's ale-taster or ale-conner, an official appointed to enforce the regulations regarding price and measure. The brewster, when she had a batch of ale ready to sell, would supposedly advertise the fact by hoisting a staff with a leafy bough attached to it – the "ale-stake" – outside her house. This would also alert the ale-taster. (Although for more on the subject of ale-stakes, see Appendix I).

Brewing for a Living

Given the variables, the actual profitability of medieval brewing is extremely difficult to determine, even where the price of grain is known. To give an idea of the potential, Bennett creates the hypothetical example of a brewster buying a bushel each of wheat, barley, and oats at Oxford market in November 1310, brewing 7½ gallons per bushel, and selling at 1¼d a gallon. After deducting all other expenses including firewood, the legal profit would have been less than 5d, which even in 1310 was not very much – less than two days' pay for a labourer, in fact. And there were not many ways for the brewster to cut costs, either: using a higher proportion of cheaper grains such as oats was one option; brewing weaker beer by adding more water to the mash – eight gallons per bushel seems to have been pretty standard, but it could be stretched to 10 or even 12 – was another. But in a competitive market where there were many brewsters vying for the same custom, churning out poor-quality ale and charging the full legal price for it can hardly have been a very successful long-term strategy.

Playing the market was one way of maintaining profitability. Village ale-tasters, says Bennett, tended to set the maxima that could be charged only once or twice a year. The price of grain might well fluctuate between times; if it fell, brewing for sale would be more profitable, but if it rose, the effort would have hardly been worthwhile and the brewster might have to stop working and wait for better times. To prevent this very ploy, however, local authorities could insist on brewsters continuing to brew even when a profit was all but unattainable – after all, ale was a staple and people had to have it, profit or no profit. Seen in this light, brewing for sale "within the assize" can hardly have been viable; but that's still a long way from demonstrating that the assize was a *de facto* tax. Nevertheless, the very existence of price controls was to have serious implications for the development of the alehouse, as we shall see.

For the historian, the fact that so many villagers were obliged to troop in and out of court for selling outside the assize provides a treasure-trove of records of enormous value to explore; and Bennett is undoubtedly the Amundsen of these explorers, having examined in great depth the manorial court records of more than 30 parishes, mainly in the Midlands and the East. They contain almost no suggestion that country alewives operating before the late 14th century were routinely brewing for consumption on the premises, and Bennett cites only two intriguing hints to the contrary. There are odd references to sales *in domo et extra domo*, which she takes as evidence of "rudimentary alehouses"; and there was a prosecution arising from a brawl at a *tabernus* at Wye, Kent, in 1311. But both are ambiguous. *In domo et extra domo* does not necessarily mean inside and outside the brewster's house, "*in*" in Latin also having the sense of "at". They could equally mean off-sales either direct from the brewster's own house or door-to-door via the regrators or hucksters whom we know to have existed from various sources, especially William Langland's Piers the Ploughman. And as for that *tabernus* at Wye: well, *tabernus* did not necessarily mean tavern as we understand the term. Its literal meaning is simply "box", and it was commonly used to refer to temporary booths set up at fairs and markets (Wye had had a weekly market since 1225) or on other public occasions: (church ales, although one-off events rather than permanent institutions, are routinely recorded in Latin as *tabernae ecclesiasticae*). So although the two references cited by Bennett might be taken to indicate the existence of country alehouses in the early 14th century, they are far from conclusive.

There is one unambiguous reference from the early 14th century, however, to drinking on the premises in a rural context. The Calendar of Chancery warrants for the year 1306 records a homicide in a tavern in the Hampshire village of Kelmeston (whose market had been chartered in 1254). Two men, Richard Squibes and Thomas Smel, were arguing in a tavern when Smel drew his knife and chased Squibes first out of the building and then back in. Cornered, Squibes drew his own knife and stabbed Smel to death. (He got off). Unambiguous as this reference is, though, it tells us infuriatingly little about the "tavern" where the fight occurred. Of course, it can't have been a mere stall or kiosk. But was it a permanent, fully commercial, establishment where drinking on the premises took place regularly? Or were patrons only welcome to drink indoors on market day? Given the economic crises of the times (the early 14th century was marked by a series of appalling harvests and even localised famines), it seems likely that it was the latter, and that at this stage the alehouse was an unfamiliar institution in the countryside. For until the Black Death of 1348-49 changed everything, the economic circumstances of the peasantry as well as the social conventions of village life undermined the potential of separate, permanent, and above all commercial establishments dedicated to social drinking on the premises that we have established as defining a pub. There might have been a living of sorts to be made by brewing for sale, although only the poorest households, generally those of single woman, seem to have had brewing as their sole livelihood; but if there was a better living to be made by running an alehouse the court records don't show people exploiting it.

Competition and the Market

Perhaps because so many village women were engaged in brewing for sale, the volume each brewster could produce weighs against the idea that some of them ran proto-pubs. A typical output of around 40 gallons a week, according to Bennett's calculations, would be insufficient, once whatever quantities kept back for the household and sold for consumption off the premises were deducted, to sustain a commercial drinking establishment. Furthermore, if any of the myriad brewsters trundled before the manorial courts of medieval England had been running their homes as full-time shebeens, you would expect to find a single name or a small number of names in each village being presented at every session of the manorial court, or at almost every session, over a period of years. And although some women were indeed hauled up more often than others, this does not seem to have been the case until the Black Death wrought its many and deep social and economic changes.

The pattern of leisure in the medieval village also undermined the potential for a commercial alehouse. Working people in a medieval village lived a much more corporate or collective life than we do. They toiled alongside each other in a single great field of separate strips. They made decisions and judgements together as jurors in the manorial court. And they celebrated together at feasts, holy days, and wakes organised by the church or by craft or religious guilds. The revelries of Merrie England were much more like village fetes or street parties, centrally organised and held to mark special events or to raise money in aid of good causes or indigent or unfortunate individuals, than the casual and unstructured pubgoing of today. Furthermore, from what we know of medieval merriments they were mainly outdoor events, offering little scope for business to a proto-pub. There were indoor games suitable for winter evenings that might have been played in an alehouse, but not many of them: no playing cards yet, but "tables" (backgammon?), knucklebones, dice, and perhaps even chess. But medieval peasants and burgesses seemed to have had a greater liking for spectacle, preferably rowdy spectacle: Joseph Strutt's monumental *Sports and Pastimes of the English People* (1801) lists diversions such as mock-combat both armed and unarmed; numerous variations on putting the shot; even more numerous variations on torturing animals; and mass-participation football such as survives in Ashbourne, Derbyshire, and Haxey near Doncaster to this very day. For the less violently inclined, cambuca was an early version either of cricket or golf or quite possibly both; quoits and bowls were both popular; and (to judge from various marginalia), both exhibition and participation dances were extraordinarily vigorous (as witness the exertions involved in modern morris dancing). Religious festivals, too, tended towards the spectacular, often being marked by pageants, processions, and parades, while the "mystery" plays staged by religious and trade guilds (or "misteries") were generally bawdier than their subject matter might suggest.

Then there were events such as scot-ales ("scot" meaning tax, in which sense it survives in the expression "scot-free") and bid-ales that were quite openly intended to raise money, sometimes for the upkeep of the church, but often with no religious significance. Attendance was in many cases compulsory, especially when the proceeds were earmarked for the church, and alewives were often forbidden to brew in competition with them. There were a great many of them, too – as many as 90 a year in the calendars of most villages – and, hard as peasant life may have been, not all these excuses for riotous leisure were necessarily all that welcome. The 1217 Charter of the Forest, which reformed and softened the savage forest laws of the Normans, actually forbade the foresters from holding quasi-official scot-ales that seem to have been no more than opportunities for semi-official extortion (although since the foresters had to be reined in again in 1279 the original charter seems not to have been all that well enforced. Hardly surprising, since the people who were supposed to enforce it were the foresters themselves!). Such festivities could last several days and involve copious drinking: at the annual scot-ale held in the Deverills in Wiltshire, bachelors were entitled to as much free ale as they could hold on the final day – provided they drank it standing up (Clark). Weddings and funerals were also occasions for festivities at which specially-brewed ale was sold either to help the newlyweds on their way, or to support the relicts of the deceased. The frequency and duration of these events and entertainments provoked later Puritan writers to complain that they tempted servants and labourers away from their duties for days on end and left them unfit for work for some time after; but their importance to us is that they stood in the place of, even in the way of, the commercial potential of a recognisable alehouse.

Finally, there were too many competing sources of free ale to make a village alehouse a commercial proposition. We cannot know how many households brewed their own beer, since domestic production was not recorded in official documents such as court rolls; but there is reason to suppose it was substantial. In well-off households, live-in servants got a generous ration of ale as part of their board. And feudal tenants spent much of their time – two or three days a week, in many cases – working on the lord's land, when they were commonly fed and watered at the lord's expense. Every quart or pottle of ale handed out free to customary labourers by the lord's bailiff was a potential sale denied to the alehouse keeper.

Not only do court records, patterns of leisure, and competing sources of ale point away from pre-Plague brewsters running full-time on-trade establishments, but how many of their customers could have afforded to patronise such proto-pubs? In the late 13th century, according to Peter Clark, a gallon of the cheapest ale cost about a third of a skilled craftsmen's daily wage, or two-thirds that of a journeyman. For the poor, as William Langland's *The Vision of Piers Plowman* protests, ale was a luxury even after the general increase in disposable that followed the Black Death (a subject to which we shall return). Nor would there have been much in the way of passing trade to swell the ranks of the alewife's potential customers. Travellers might have bought ale as they passed: Chaucer's Pardoner (a generation after the watershed of the Black Death, it should be noted) insisted before starting his tale: "Here at this ale-stake/I will bothe drynke and byten on a cake". But a customer like the Pardoner can only have been a rare windfall for the pre-Plague alewife: outside the principal towns, where commercial inns were established as early as the 13th century, bed and board for the wayfarer were generally provided by charity. Monastic *hospitia* or guesthouses we shall encounter in a later chapter. Many town corporations and guilds also ran hostels, mainly for pilgrims, known as *Maisons Dieux*; and hospitality was also commonly offered in the halls of castles and baronial households. All of these institutions, whether pious, public, or merely hospitable, can only have soaked up the demand that might otherwise have made alehouses a viable proposition.

The Best Third

But if the likeliest (if not perhaps definitive) interpretation of the evidence is that the alehouse as a separate, defined, and permanent establishment where customers habitually drank on the premises simply didn't exist in English villages before the mid-14th century, some of the groundwork for its eventual appearance had been laid by an amendment to the Assize of Bread and Ale.

In the modern world, pub prices are higher than supermarket prices because of the publican's greater proportional investment in staff and facilities. Today the price differential, however damaging it is to the pub trade, is more or less accepted; but the 1267 assize allowed no such variation, and since it was a codification or consolidation of the many local assizes of the previous century one might assume that they didn't either. This implies two things: first, that the three successively weaker mashes from the same charge of malt were expected to be blended together before sale; and second, that the quality of the ale – that is, the proportion of different grains used in each grist and the amount of water added to the grist – was determined entirely by the market. So, when there was money about, brewsters could compete by producing the best ale in the village; and when times were lean they could try to turn a profit by brewing as cheaply as they could get away with. The retail price, however, remained the same.

The 1276 amendment to the Assize allowed brewsters to charge slightly more for the "best" ale – but it's not stated what is meant by "best". It could mean that the product of the first and strongest of the three mashes might be sold separately from the other two; or it could have been an incentive for the brewster to produce better-quality ale by improving her chances of making a reasonable margin on it. Given that complaints about the former practice persisted for well over a century afterwards, and that (as Bennett reveals) many village alewives brewed fairly substantial quantities to supply the local gentry who might be expected to insist on quality, the latter possibility seems perhaps the likeliest (although it's entirely possible that the unspecified offence of "selling outside the assize" before the 1276 amendment might usually have referred to the practice of selling the first mash separately at a much higher price). But the important point, as far as the eventual emergence of the alehouse is concerned, is that the concept of differential pricing was established. The commodification of ale was undermined, and customers gradually became conditioned to the idea of paying more for better.

Market conditions, though, were not yet right for a village alewife to make the transition into a pub landlady. There was still too much competition for not enough trade. Many writers, even quite august ones, have simply assumed that there were alehouses, or prototypes of alehouses, in the countryside of late 13th-century England. But while it might easily be possible (and in the case of Kelmeston is confirmed) that some customers of some brewsters sometimes drank their quart of ale (not all that much more than a modern pint, remember) before leaving a brewery that was also a neighbour's kitchen... well, that's quite some distance from the definition of a pub set out in the introduction.

CHAPTER 4: GUILDHALLS & MARKET STALLS

Having looked for the roots of the Great British Pub in the countryside of Olde England and failed to find them there it's time to turn our attention to the towns, and to one town in particular: London. But before we venture into the narrow filth-strewn streets and alleyways of the Square Mile, we do need to take a look back at Rome. Yes, the link Hackwood sought to establish between the institutions of medieval England and those of ancient Rome is, as we now know, spurious. Nevertheless, since the Romans do seem to have invented the tavern the least we can do is visit.

Bars, Brothels and Casinos of Ancient Rome

The Romans habitually led much of their social lives in public. Wealthy citizens, as Petronius and many others tell us, were great and indeed highly competitive home entertainers, and the dinner-party menus of the rich and powerful reached quite ludicrous heights of exotic elaboration. But working Romans appear to have eaten out a great deal in *thermopolia*, perhaps best described as cookshops, of which more than 150 have been excavated in Pompeii alone, with still more in Herculaneum and Ostia.

Thermopolia came in all sizes from fairly humble shop-fronts to much grander establishments with dining-rooms at the back and even, in some cases, letting rooms upstairs. The feature common to all *thermopolia* was a long counter of marble or stone perforated with holes in which *dolia*, or large earthenware jars, were set. Exactly what these jars contained is still a matter for conjecture. It might have been wine; it might have been cold food; or it might have been hot food.

The problem with interpreting these *dolia* is that they appear to have been fixtures, concreted permanently in place, which would have made effective cleaning all but impossible. The best guess must be, therefore, that they were wine-jars, and that the hot food that gave this class of establishment its name – including chickpea pottage, sausages (*tomacula*), and the rather alarmingly-named *botuli*, or blood puddings – was cooked on a separate stove. Citizens of all ranks commonly took their *prandium* or midday meal at work, buying their food at *thermopolia* either to eat in or take away. But by night the nature and clientele of these establishments changed. Many of them, judging from surviving frescoes and graffiti, also operated as brothels or casinos; and we read in Juvenal's *Satires* that Romans of all ranks from the dissolute consul Lateranus to his low-life cohort of assassins, sailors, thieves, runaway slaves and (rather oddly) coffin-makers enjoyed each others' company at all-night drinking bouts in the *thermopolia* of Ostia.

But what of the *tabernae* or stalls, from which the word "tavern" itself immediately derives? Although they have left no physical remains for the simple reason that they were made of wood, we know from Martial's *Epigrams* and other sources that they were commonplace, even ubiquitous, lining the main streets of Rome itself and also, presumably, those of other cities. They became such an obstructive nuisance that the Emperor Domitian tried to ban them. But were *tabernae* pubs? The word literally means box or booth; and to a Roman a *taberna* was no more than a semi-permanent kiosk that might be occupied, so Martial tells us, by a range of street traders including pastry-cooks, butchers, hair-dressers, and apothecaries as well as wine sellers. There's certainly no suggestion that they were on-trade premises where social drinking went on; but the very fact that the word was adopted by early medieval scribes to mean drinking establishments is telling, as we shall see.

If the *taberna* probably doesn't fit the model of a pub we established in the Introduction, then the *thermopolium* – or at least, the kind of *thermopolium* where Lateranus drank his nights away amid the common people – probably does. We have to be careful, though, of the tendency to try to trace the roots of modern institutions as far back as they will go for fear of going even further. As we now understand, urban life in Britain disappeared along with its economic underpinnings following the collapse of Roman power, Canterbury being one possible survivor. If the cities were gone, though, they weren't forgotten. The physical presence of their ruins ensured that; and they were still visible enough three centuries later to provide the premise of one of the best-known meditative poems of the Anglo-Saxon era, *The Ruin*. In fact just two words in *The Ruin* have been taken by many as the reason why the Saxons didn't, at first, resettle old Roman sites: according to the poem, the derelict city was "*enta geweorc*", the work of giants – and therefore haunted and far too frightening (so the reasoning goes) for hyper-superstitious Saxons to live in.

In reality, the Saxons were perfectly familiar with Roman cities, their ancestors having fought both alongside and against Roman armies for generations. The reason why they didn't immediately resettle the *ceastres* was probably more prosaic and practical than any fear of ghostly giants. Rather than waste time and labour in clearing tons of fallen masonry and breaking through stone pavements and foundations to dig the post-holes for their wooden huts and halls, they built on greenfield sites just outside the ancient walls, thus exploiting the old cities' locational advantages but for a fraction of the effort of recolonising them. In some cases they even used a particular and significant Latin suffix to name their settlements: a *vicus* was a civilian village and trading post founded alongside a legionary fortress. It transliterates into Old English as "*-wic*"; hence the name of the settlement that sprang up in about the year 500 – judging by the dating of the oldest piece of pottery found on the site – just to the west of one particular derelict Roman city, on the bend of the Thames where the Strand and Covent Garden are today: Lundenwic.

Anglo-Saxon London

Given the advantages of its location, Lundenwic flourished. According to the Venerable Bede's *Historia Ecclesiastica*, completed in about 730, it was already the chief town (he uses the word "metropolis") of the East Saxons when in 604 it was chosen by St Augustine to be the seat of a bishop, Mellitus. Mellitus didn't last long: he was ousted when the East Saxons reverted to paganism in 616, and Lundenwic didn't have another bishop until St Eorconweald in 675. But coinage appears to have returned in the mid-7th century; and from the 670s trade through the city is mentioned in the royal records of its neighbouring kingdoms, Kent, Surrey, and Mercia. Bede also reports the presence of Frisian slave-traders in 679, when he says London was "an emporium for many nations". From the middle of the 8th century there are signs of occupation in the old Roman city; but the repopulation of the former Londinium didn't really get under way until the Viking invasions of the mid-9th century, when its still-formidable fortifications once again proved their worth. Lundenwic was unsuccessfully attacked in 842 and again in 851, and only in 871 did it fall to a Viking army led by Ivar the Boneless. Alfred the Great and his brother-in-law, Ealdorman Ethelred of West Mercia, drove Ivar out in 886 and Ethelred appears to have ruled the city until his death in 911. But with the boundary of the Danelaw on the River Lea only four miles to the east, Lundenwic was now as much a garrison town as an entrepôt – a change reflected in the adoption of a new name, Lundenburgh.

Under Earl Ethelred's energetic rule, Londinium was refounded. A new wharf and market, Queenhithe (possibly originally Cornhithe or Quernhithe), was chartered in 889, to be followed in the 10th century by Billingsgate. The ancient walls were repaired, with a new encircling ditch. Southwark, deserted since around 400, was rebuilt as a fortified burgh, perhaps protecting the southern end of a new bridge that may have built at around this time. After Ethelred's death King Edward the Elder, Alfred the Great's redoubtable son, took personal control of London and went on the offensive, recapturing East Anglia and the Danish half of Mercia. No longer a military outpost on a dangerous frontier, London was free to flourish. Lundenwic and Lundenburgh insensibly merged; the separate names gradually disappeared (although an echo of Lundenwic survives to this day as Aldwych); and the rebuilding of Londinium began in earnest on a new grid of gravelled streets based round a great *ceap* or market. The wharves and market attracted colonies of foreign merchants, many of them from the recently-converted Scandinavian countries: thus the descendants of the great plunderers became the pious founders of St Clement Danes and other London churches. By the late 10th century the city was home to merchants from Germany, Flanders, and Northern France, too, importing wine, timber, and wool.

Inevitably such a wealthy and populous city attracted royal attention. The family seat of the House of Wessex – often, but anachronistically, described as their capital – was Winchester; but Edward the Elder's son Athelstan convened several royal councils in London and established eight moneyers there in the early years of his reign. In the renewed Viking wars that plagued the long reign of Ethelred the Unready (978-1016) London was a key strategic target for the invaders but held true to the royal dynasty under which its fortune had been made: three times the Danes attacked; three times the Londoners fought them off. On their fourth attempt, in 1014, the invaders took the city and forced Ethelred briefly into exile: after his return, recapturing it was his first priority. A measure of its wealth, even after more than a generation of warfare, is that in 1018 it paid King Canute £10,500 of a national levy of £83,000. Edward the Confessor continued London's gradual transformation into a royal city with the refounding of St Peter's Abbey on Thorney Island in his later years: as Westminster Abbey it hosted the first of 37 coronations (so far) a few days after Edward's death, when Harold II briefly seized the throne. The process was taken forward by Harold's vanquisher William I with the building of the Tower of London as a royal fortress and completed by William Rufus with the establishment of the Palace of Whitehall in 1097 as a royal residence and administrative HQ.

By the time of the Conquest London had perhaps 15-20,000 inhabitants; its nearest rival, York, trailed with fewer than 10,000. Princes and prelates, merchants and magnates rubbed shoulders with hawkers and hucksters as they went about their business in its bustling streets. But what did they do when business was finished for the day? Had they no pubs to go to?

One thing we have established about the Anglo-Saxons was that they liked to party: the royal feast and the great hall in which it was held are as central to *Beowulf* as the characters and the plot. We know a certain amount about procedures at these carousals, as well: remnants of harps have been found, and dice, and knucklebones; songs, poems for recital, and riddles survive in great number. We even know of a drinking game, drinking at pins, in which nails were fixed at set intervals into the side of a beer-mug which would be passed round: the players had to drink accurately from one nail to the next – presumably with a forfeit if they drank too much or too little. St Dunstan's 12th-century biographer William of Malmesbury sought to spin this as a way of preventing excessive drinking: the saint, he claimed, had ordained the fixing of nails (*clavos*) at set intervals so that every drinker could gauge how much to swig at one time. It sounds slightly impractical, but it does at least tell us that passing round a mug or cup (*vasus*) was part of the drinking ritual. The ninth canon of the orders issued after the Council of London (1102), though, confirms the true nature of the practice, ordering priests not to attend drinking-bouts or to drink at pins ("*ut presbyteri non eant ad potationes nec ad pinnos bibant*"). So the Saxons of London undoubtedly enjoyed their wine, mead, ale and *beor* as much as their country cousins did. But – and returning to the question of *potationes* – where, and in what circumstances, did they enjoy it?

Taverns or Trestles?

The first thing we need to do is clear our minds of the image of Lateranus and his cronies debauching in *thermopolia*. The stews and dives of Roman towns and cities depended on a cash economy which was not a feature of early Anglo-Saxon England. Here, the basic unit of society was the kindred group and the focus of the kindred group was its hall, where cheer was freely dispensed. There is no reason to suppose that the first inhabitants of Lundenwic and other comparable settlements made any different arrangement. There are hints, too, that it persisted as these settlements blossomed into true towns. Certainly the 8th-century poet of *The Ruin* regarded "*meodoheall monig mondreama full*" – many a meadhall full of the joys of men – as normal features of a thriving city. And once old Londinium was resettled, jurisdiction over many enclaves (indicated today by street and ward names ending in haw – *haga* – or bury – *burgh*) was granted to ecclesiastic or aristocratic magnates with judicial rights and special privileges administered through private courts that can only have been convened in the same sort of halls that were the focal points of their provincial estates.

But urban life has a way of undermining traditional patterns of communal life and hierarchy, especially where those patterns are based on kinship. As the city filled up with deracinated migrants – both workers coming in from the surrounding countryside and merchants from all over Northern Europe – many if not most of the inhabitants must have found themselves with no kindred groups to belong to and no lords to attach themselves to. But one of the recurrent themes of Anglo-Saxon poetry is the importance of belonging, and so Londoners began to fill the gap left by their missing kindred groups by forming guilds with peacekeeping, religious, and even military functions, such as the *cnichtengild* based in what is now Portsoken ward. The guild structure survived the Conquest; and although we know little of how Saxon guilds were organised and administered, one thing we can reasonably assume is that each one had as its headquarters a hall to host social and religious functions as well as official business.

The pace and pattern of life was moving on, though. A communal hall where the villagers, or the kindred, or the local aristocracy, could meet on a more or less formal basis to transact official business, to celebrate saints' days, to join together for seasonal feasts, or simply for family meals, was rather left behind by the far more flexible and fluid nature of urban life. People whose work might take them all over the city, and whose daily schedule was no longer governed by the rising and setting of the sun, might need victualling on the move and at any time of day or night. Many of them might not even be clients or members of the magnates or guilds and might not therefore have access to their halls. Many of them would be transient visitors to the city or semi-resident foreign merchants.

It might be assumed, even if it cannot be proved, that the bread and ale provided in the kindred halls of Old English villages were baked and brewed by the kindred for the kindred, that all members made do with whatever was put on the communal table, and that no money changed hands. This was certainly not so in London, or at least, not for everybody. The heart of the recolonised city was its great *ceap* or market, where cash was king. And there was cash about, too, plenty of the good silver pennies of whose quality the later Saxon and Anglo-Danish kings were so jealous. As long ago as the late 8th century King Offa of Mercia had standardised the pennyweight at 22 grains; and in his long reign Ethelred the Unready was able to collect 40 million of them to pay the Danegeld. And this is where a new word enters the language – or, at least, an old word re-enters it; and the word is tavern.

As it ever was and probably ever shall be – and fortunately for us – this rediscovered word was from the outset clouded by plumes of official disapproval. Fortunate, that is, because it means the word was written down. Throughout the 9th, 10th and 11th centuries, Anglo-

Saxon abbots and bishops fired salvo after salvo of stern admonitions against clergy who lived too much in the world: marrying, working, bearing arms -- and drinking. They were meant to be a priestly caste, above the glee-singing, the story-telling, and the recitals of profane poetry that accompanied the feasting in the meadhall. And they should not, as more earthly people did, frequent taverns. "*Ut sacerdos ebriatum et tabernas fugiat,*" thundered one canonical injunction ("Let the priest shun drunkenness and the tavern."). "*Ut nullus presbyter edendi vel bibendi causa in tabernis!*" cried another. ("No priest ought to eat or drink at a tavern," although it charitably added "*nisi peregrationis necessitate compulsi*", unless forced by the necessities of travel.)

In considering these repeated episcopal fulmin-ations, though, we always need to take an important caveat into account. Across the Frankish empire and its successor states, zealous reformers were continually striving to bring the expanding and unwieldy church under closer control, with the morals, manners, and social standing of the clergy a particular focus of concern. Many of the decrees issued in England against priestly drunkenness, and against the use of *taberni* in particular, were copied almost word for word from capitularies promulgated in the Frankish states; one at least was transcribed from the late Roman Third Council of Carthage, which took place in 397! Even the often-cited admonitory preamble to the law-code of Alfred the Great's penalising damage to a neighbour's vines, which has often been taken to imply widespread viticulture in late 9th-century England, turns out on closer inspection to have been lifted from Exodus, an appeal to Scripture being fundamental to any self-respecting Christian king's legislation. So how closely these railings against priestly sottishness *in tabernis* mirrored the actual situation on the ground is open to question.

For the Frankish states of the 10th century were very different from Anglo-Saxon England. By the time the Franks overran the provinces of Germany and Gaul they were, unlike the Anglo-Saxons, already

Christian and pretty thoroughly Romanised; and the cities they conquered, unlike the cities the Saxons disdained to settle, were no mere shells. Aachen, Cologne, Metz, Trier – these had been the military and financial headquarters of Emperors since the third century when the barbarian threat to the Rhine frontier first materialised. By the 5th century they might not have been exactly flourishing but were still very much in being, and the Franks took them alive. So when a Frankish bishop inveighed against priests who were too fond of tavern life, he was speaking literally rather than metaphorically. In fact in 910 or thereabouts when Regino of Prüm, Abbot of St Martin's at Trier, compiled a list of questions bishops should ask of local priests when making their official visitations, question 23 was "*si in tabernis hibat?*" (does he hang out at taverns?); while question 27 was "*si calicem aut patenam vel vestimentum sacerdotale aut librum praesumat tabernario vel negotiatori in vadum dari?*" (has he pawned the church plate, vestments, or books to a tavern-keeper or merchant?).

But what were these establishments that English priests needed to avoid? The choice of the word *tabernus* is a strong clue that we are back in Martial's Rome where wooden booths – market stalls, in effect – lined the streets selling anything from a haircut to a sausage and including a cup of wine. A Frankish *tabernarius* who was also functioning as a pawnbroker might be running a business that was rather more substantial than a trestle-table in the street; but the impression that the *taberni* of Anglo-Saxon London, if perhaps not those of Aachen, Cologne, Metz and Trier, were street kiosks rather than indoor bars is reinforced by the occasionally-seen Old English word that describes them – *ceapælepel*, from *ceap* meaning market, *ælu* meaning of course ale, and *piling* meaning a board or trestle. It sounds more like a place where one goes to buy ale and perhaps a dish of sausages to take away than a place to consume them in.

Nevertheless, and even if the *ceapælepel* was not quite a pub, an important step had been taken along the road to the birth of the pub.

That tiny fraction of Englishmen who lived in London had got the idea that a drink was something you could have whenever you wanted – not necessarily to celebrate the harvest, nor to toast the thegn's birthday, nor even round the communal table of the kindred hall, but for no better reason than that you fancied one and had the money to pay for it.

We have already encountered the decree issued by Ethelred the Unready in the closing years of the 10th century that fixes the fines for brawling in the *æla huse*. It may very well be that the deracinated inhabitants of London, whether merchants or migrant labourers, had started to compensate for the much-missed comradeship of the ancestral kindred hall by frequenting establishments that you or I might just recognise as a pub. For although what texts we possess, taken individually, don't yet describe anything more substantial than an open-fronted kiosk, taken together they indicate strongly that the habit of purely social drinking was catching on in an increasingly cosmopolitan city where there was more than enough cash circulating to make full-time ale-selling a viable commercial proposition. We cannot say that pre-Conquest Londoners had an Ethelred's Head or King Alfred's Arms to go to; indeed, to judge solely from the surviving written records, opening time was still some generations in the future. And when the *tabernus* was finally ready to leave the market-place and move indoors out of the weather, the change came from an unexpected direction.

CHAPTER 5: ASSEMBLING IN TAVERNS

At some point in the late 11th or very early 12th century a new social amenity was added to the guildhalls and *caepælepel* of Norman London: the pub – or something very like it.

The Council of London that in 1102 denounced the game of drinking at pins also denounced priests who went "*ad potationes*" – to drinking-bouts. We know a little of the nature of these *potationes* – or perhaps *beorscipe?* – from Bede's tale of Caedmon and his Life of St Oswald; but not nearly enough, and from an entirely different context. In the city, where the ties of kinship were broken, when might *potationes* be held, and by whom? Were they formal celebrations, or impromptu booze-ups? Were they free or paid for? Were they held in private homes or public halls? The council's decree gives us no clue.

William of Malmesbury, though, writing in 1126, is more obliging. Attempting to spin drinking at pins as a temperance measure decreed by St Dunstan rather than the drinking game it surely was, William tells us in his *Gesta Pontificum Anglorum*:

"*In tantum et in frivolis pacis sequax, ut quia compatriotae in tabernis convenientes, jamque temulenti pro modo bibendi contenderent, ipse clavos argenteos vel aureos jusserit vasis affigi ut dum metam suam quisque cognosceret non plus subserviente verecundia, vel ipse appeteret, vel alium appetere cogeret.*" (So anxious was he to keep the peace even in small matters that, as his countrymen used to assemble in taverns and when excited would quarrel as to how much they could hold, he ordered gold or silver pegs to be fastened in their drinking bowls, so that while every man knew his capacity, he would be ashamed either to take more himself, or oblige others to drink more than their limit.)

"*In tabernis convenientes*": assembling at or in taverns. This may not have been an accurate description of the social life of the priests of St Dunstan's day more than 150 years earlier, but clearly "assembling at or in taverns" was something that William was familiar with, even though he lived in seclusion as librarian of Malmesbury Abbey in rural Wiltshire. But what did he mean by "taverns"? Not halls, clearly. But, to my mind, not mere booths either. For although he doesn't say so explicitly, the context suggests that the assembling was more "in" than "at". It's hard to imagine the sort of drinking-bout William is talking about being held in the street at an outdoor market stall, a *caepælepel*. It's surely an indoor activity, and strongly suggests that by his time taverns were not only takeaways but were also places where people could gather.

Alas, though: as with the single unequivocal mention of the late 10th-century *æla huse,* this is an isolated notice and we don't meet the word tavern again for another fifty years (not in England, at least, although that famous German Goliard drinking song, *Meum est in tabernum propositum mori* – I plan to die in a tavern – dates from the 1160s). Thereafter, though, the word occurs with increasing frequency. In 1175 Richard of Dover, Beckett's successor as Archbishop of Canterbury, convened another council intended to address the question of clerical regulation and behaviour. One of its canons, that against priestly drunkenness, was more or less a reissue of the 1102 injunction – except that to the word *potationes* it added a new one, *taberni*. The formula was repeated 20 years later at the Council of York convened by Richard of Dover's successor, Hubert Walter; and it might be supposed that these canonical injunctions were, as so often, merely reusing the same form of words without actually taking into account the reality on the ground. But at about the same time as the Council of York there came an important text which, with a little reading between the lines, seems to confirm the existence of taverns or something very like them.

Down by the Riverside

The *Description of London* was written in about 1190 by William Fitzstephen, Thomas Becket's biographer and former secretary whom we have already met extolling Becket's diplomatic gift of fine ale to the King of France. Fitzstephen describes cookshops (*publica coquina*) and taverns (*cellis vinariis venalia,* literally "vintners' retail cellars") lining the riverfront, which was evidently a pretty lively part of town. "There every day, according to the season," says Fitzstephen, "may be found meat of every kind, roast, fried, and boiled; fish both large and small; coarse meat for the poor and more delicate for the rich – venison, poultry, gamebirds. If friends, tired after their journey, should arrive unexpectedly at a citizen's house and, being hungry, don't want to wait for fresh meat to be bought and cooked ... someone will run down to the riverside and instantly get anything they might want". This doesn't seem to suggest a restaurant so much as a giant takeaway; and indeed the word tavern was only interpolated when the *Description* was first translated as an appendix to John Stow's *Survey of London* more than 400 years later. But then Fitzstephen adds, almost as an afterthought, that soldiers and pilgrims passing through the city and stopping at the cookshop had delicacies placed before them (*appositis ... deliciis*"). In other words, the cookshops were more than just takeaways: they were restaurants where it was possible to eat in. Add to that the *cellis vinariis venalia* nearby and the wharves begin to resemble a primordial soup in which all or almost all the ingredients of a pub are floating around, waiting for the catalyst that will bring them together. And that catalyst, in a sense, was homesickness.

In the aftermath of the Conquest, London experienced an unprecedented surge of immigration as Norman and Northern French carpetbaggers scrambled to share out the booty. There had, of course, been foreign merchants in the city before, but in small numbers and, for the most part, transient. Even as late as the 14th century, according to Stephen Inwood (*A History of London*, Macmillan 1998), London's population of Italian merchants numbered only 70, while The Steelyard, now buried under Cannon Street Station but then the semi-fortified base of the Baltic traders of the mighty Hanseatic League, was home to a mere 20 souls. But some 20,000 Norman settlers and their households are estimated to have followed in the Conqueror's wake. London's population at the time numbered about 1% of the national total, and if the immigrants had settled proportionately around the country then the city would suddenly have found itself host to 200 or so well-off Norman families. This in itself would have been a considerable influx. Undoubtedly, though, London was the honey-pot and must have attracted more than its fair share of incomers. Exactly how numerous the Norman and French community was we can't know; but in a city of no more than 15-20,000 it must have been a very significant new element.

New émigrés, as we know from the everyday experience of any modern city, tend to stick together, to speak their own language with their own countrymen, and to recreate, if they can, a little bit of home. To this natural urge was added the need for security, for the new Norman burgesses, powerful though they were, were still heavily outnumbered by a hostile population whose language they couldn't even understand. The migrants had arrived suddenly in a city that was wholly unprepared for them and had no facilities for them; they therefore had to construct all the social institutions that bind and identify a community for themselves, and in short order. But where, in this foreign city, might they find a place they could call their own?

There was one quarter of London where few natives (now that the Old English élite had been largely displaced) would have had occasion to go but which Normans and Frenchmen must have visited all the time, and that was The Vintry, the cluster of late Saxon wharves dated by archaeologists to the late 10th-early 11th centuries around what is now the northern foot of Southwark Bridge. Here wine was landed, and here Fitzstephen's *cellis vinariis venalia* dealt in the one commodity the incomers craved but their unwilling hosts could not provide. Insensibly, perhaps, these cellars became the invaders' social gathering-places as customers tasting the wines they were about to buy lingered to chat with fellow French-speakers. Perhaps, one day, one of the tasters sent out to a neighbouring *coquina* for something solid to soak up the wine, and the tasting session stretched out into a long afternoon's booze-up – the first, perhaps, of many. Eventually an exasperated vintner decided that these "tasting" sessions were costing him a fortune and started charging. In time, as more and more homesick Frenchmen dropped by for a cup of wine and stayed for a second and then a third, on-sales became as great a source of revenue as off-sales; and there, in a wine-cellar off what is now Upper Thames Street, probably in the late 11th century, the Great British Pub was born. Of course, I can't prove that wine-merchants' cellars morphed into taverns; but there is a well-documented parallel from the 17th century when farriers would sell a pint of home-brew to the customers whose horses they were shoeing. In many cases they found that beer sales were worth more than blacksmithing and made the transition from forge to pub – hence the great number of pubs with a "horseshoe" component in their names. The mishaps outlined in the popular ballad *The Industrious Blacksmith* suggest that this was not necessarily a wise decision!

As to when this process occurred, I would suggest an early date. It would be the first generation or two of immigrants who felt most isolated and insecure, and it seems to me likeliest that the process of evolution from wine-merchant to taverner started quite quickly after 1066. A remark of William of Malmesbury's, that in England the hitherto frugal and austere Norman and French conquerors learnt the vices of dissipation and drunkenness (from the English, he says), might be taken as supporting the idea that they had more access to liquor than their forbears did. Perhaps they were spending their time in taverns? It may be impossible to prove definitively – and for some, at least, impossible to accept – that the habit of pub-going, or at least of informal social drinking out of the home, was not an English innovation at all but was the creation of uprooted Norman emigrés. But there is a strong case for it. An alternative explanation is that the Normans brought the habit with them: taverns seem to have survived the Frankish takeover of the old Roman cities of the Rhine, and Rouen, the Norman capital, was always open to Frankish influence. Rouen was very similar to London in some ways – it was a tidal inland port serving a large and wealthy hinterland – but it was more sophisticated in the sense that it was a genuine capital city with a permanent ducal palace; and it was only very slightly smaller with about 12,000 inhabitants. It may very well have had recognisable taverns, although there is no solid evidence of it. But whether the habit of pub-going was brought over the sea or coalesced around the wine-merchants' cellars of The Vintry, it was almost certainly a Norman innovation.

And it seems to have remained a Norman habit for quite some time, for detailed research has revealed that the new elite stood aloof and separate from the natives for much longer than was previously thought. Saving the aristocracy, who lived almost in a bubble of their own, it was always believed that further down the social scale the native and French populations started fusing quite quickly after the Conquest. This has been disproved by the Oxford prosopographist Katharine Keats-Rohan, whose detailed study of 2,000 Norman families in the century following the Conquest found that only 5% intermarried with native families during the first four generations (*Domesday People*, Boydell Press 1999). Perhaps it was a certain chauvinism among the English – a disdain of the Frenchified habits of their wine-drinking masters – that held English ale-brewers back from opening their doors and English ale-drinkers from demanding to be allowed in. More likely it was a question of economics, for even in London brewing appears to have yielded only slim pickings. But whatever the reason, more than a century was to pass before the alehouse proper emerged from the murk. And when it did come along, it was such a novelty that there wasn't even a word for it.

Alehouse Economics

A census carried out by the Court of Common Council on St Valentine's Day 1309 counted 354 taverns in London and 1,334 *braciatores* or brewers. This sounds straightforward enough, except that we don't really know what it means. Were all the taverns wine-taverns, or did some of them sell ale? Were the *braciatores* brewers pure and simple, or did all or some or perhaps none of them run alehouses as well? Were they all male or were some of them actually *braciatrices* – female brewers – operating under their husbands' names and perhaps, like their country cousins, only brewing from time to time?

However that bald statistic breaks down, it does point to one conclusion: that the economics of brewing in early 14th-century London must have been extraordinarily difficult; for in a population estimated at 80,000 that number of *braciatores* is nothing short of astonishing. It averages out at one per 60 inhabitants, male and female, young and old. Such a ratio might not have been unusual in a village like Brigstock in Northamptonshire, where Judith M Bennett found that a quarter of the village women paid fines at one time or another for brewing "out of the assize". But for a 13th and 14th-century countrywoman brewing for sale was often an expedient when funds were short rather than a full-time occupation, while in London brewing was already evolving from a craft to an industry. Although the Brewers' Company was not chartered until 1437, a guild of brewers had first entered the record books in 1312 when it (unsuccessfully) sought permission for members to extract water from the Chepe conduit. Clearly the overheads of a full-time brewery must have been very much higher than those of an alewife brewing for domestic consumption in her own kitchen and producing a surplus for sale as need arose; and the profits represented the brewer's principal source of income rather than a little cash on the side.

Given an average consumption of a (medieval) gallon per head per day (although this long-accepted estimate has recently been challenged by Martyn Cornell, who questions whether England grew enough grain to bake all the country's bread and to brew 4-5,000,000 gallons of ale a day as well), then each of London's 1,334 brewers can only have sold on average 60 gallons of ale a day. If they all sold at the permitted price of 1½d a gallon they would each have turned over only 90d a day, or £2.6s.3d a week, from which malt, fuel (very expensive in medieval London), cooperage, wages (if any), rent, and taxes would all have been deducted before there was any profit. On such slim margins it must surely have been impossible to obey the assize and survive.

One answer might have been to brew weaker beer – an avenue, however, that was in theory at least closed off by the ale-conners, who were supposed to test each brew before it went on sale. The options for most were either to ignore the permitted prices and factor the consequent fines into their budgets, as many country brewers seem to have done, or to seek ways of retailing that more or less dodged the assize.

One very common way of doing this was to use middlemen – in practice, middlewomen – known as hucksters or regrators, who would hawk the ale door-to-door and in the streets or perhaps run a market stall. Cooks and piebakers are also recorded as regrators in later years. There was no law against hucksters *per se*, provided they sold the ale in the permitted measures and at the permitted price: Rose the Regrator in Langland's *Piers Plowman* is named as both brewster and huckster. But whether the huckster was an employee who had to be paid or an independent third party who needed to make a profit on the deal, regrating can (legally) only have eaten into the brewer's margin. The method brewers most commonly adopted to protect their margin seems to have been to oblige their regrators either to overcharge or sell short measure. As a result hucksters were commonly characterised as cheating the poor and were popularly depicted – along with cheating brewsters – as destined for Hell. Misogyny, and the moralising nature of the literature in which they were thus traduced, undoubtedly played a large part in their negative portrayal, as Judith M Bennett points out; nevertheless, loved or loathed, they were evidently not uncommon in the streets of medieval London and other towns, selling a whole range of goods as well as ale; and for the brewer, they made it possible to extend the retail operation beyond the brewery doors and thus expand the volume he or she could sell. But neither option, legal or illegal, added a penny piece to the brewer's profit margin.

There was a third option that added both to volume and profit margin, and that was to throw open the brewery doors, invite the drinkers in, and sell ale in unregulated open measures: in effect, to turn the brewer's kitchen into a primitive bar. And there is good evidence that this had already started happening in the very early 13th century; although, as we have seen, the institution was so novel that it didn't even have a name.

On July 11th 1212 a great fire broke out in Southwark, burning down St Mary's Church as well as virtually all of the borough's flimsy wooden houses. Contrary winds sent the flames flaring north, razing the shops and homes on the newly-completed all-stone London Bridge, and on into the City itself, where it continued to rage. It burned for 10 days and reputedly killed 1,000 people. It was a melancholy end to the long service of London's very first Mayor, Henry Fitz Ailwin. In the year of his election, 1189, he had passed a pioneering set of building regulations intended to prevent the spread of fire. Now, 33 years later and in his last year of office, he immediately convened a meeting to enact yet stronger measures.

One clause forbade cooks and bakers, including the six *coquinae* that lined the river – Fitzstephen's cookshop(s) – from taking in lodgers. Another banned – or appeared to ban – unlicensed alehouses unless they were built of stone. Or at least, so it has always been translated. But the original Latin is worth a closer look. "*Consiliunt quod omnes scotallae defendantur, nisi de illis qui habuerint licentiam per commune consilium civitatis apud Guildhallam; praeter eos qui volunt aedificare de lapide,*" the common council decreed: "They (the councilmen) advise that all scotales should be forbidden except those who have (a) licence from the common council of the city at the Guildhall and unless they are prepared to build in stone."

First, *licentia*. This has usually been taken to mean that the Guildhall ran some sort of early licensing system. If that were true, notice of it would doubtless appear elsewhere in the reams and reams of medieval legal documents preserved in dusty archives. No such notice survives. But in classical Latin, *licentia* is one of those words – like "sanction" and "endorse" in modern English – that can carry near-opposite meanings. As well as "official permission", it can also mean exemption, or freedom from control. Senators stoutly defended their political *libertas* or privilege, while censuring the *licentia* enjoyed by the unruly mob. So *licentia* should here be taken to mean not permission, but exemption, and *nisi de illis qui habuerint licentiam per commune consilium civitatis* might be more accurately translated as "except those that have freedom from the council" – ie, those in Southwark and the other *faubourgs*, which were separate jurisdictions throughout most of the medieval period and which, ironically, is where the fire started.

Then, *scotallae*. This is universally translated as "alehouse", which in other contexts would not be at all accurate. *Scot* is simply Old English for "charge". It survives in the expression "scot-free", while the dialect word "shot", only recently obsolete, means "bill". A "scot-ale" is generally taken to mean an event at which people were expected to pay for their ale: a rent party, in modern terms. Here, though, the meaning is entirely different: *"qui volunt aedificare de lapide"* denotes a building rather than an event; and one moreover that must be built of stone because, implicitly, of the risk of fire arising from the mashing process. But not just a brewery: the usual implication of the term scot-ale is that customers drank their ale there and then rather than buying it to take home. Surely, then, the year 1212 gives us our first glimpse of the alehouse?

The linguistic ambiguity doesn't stop there, though. The first use of the English word "tavern" that I know of occurs in Robert of Gloucester's translation, in 1280-90, of Geoffrey of Monmouth's *Historia Regum Britanniae*, written 150 years earlier. In Geoffrey's version of an Arthurian episode Cador, Earl of Cornwall, surprised that soldiers who have long been idle can fight so doughtily, says: "*Quippe ubi usus armorum videtur abesse alearum vero et mulierum inflammatores caeteraque oblectamenta adesse*" – roughly, that idle soldiers tend to give themselves up to dice, womanising, and other (unspecified) pleasures. Robert of Gloucester's translation of the passage adds a detail: "*Vor wane men laeþ ydel, þat er batayles soght, her ydelnesse hem saal brynge to synne lechery, to taverne, and to sleupe, and to hassarderye*" – "for when men lie idle who once sought battle, their idleness shall bring them to the sin of lechery, to the tavern, to sloth, and to gambling." But what sort of "tavern" would the rude soldiery do their whoring and gambling in: a genteel wine bar, or a lowly alehouse? Even a century after Robert of Gloucester there is no fixed term denoting the alehouse: Langland doesn't dignify Beton the Brewster's parlour with any sort of name at all, while Chaucer at least distinguishes Absalom's haunts as taverns and brewhouses.

It's impossible to know how many of the 1,334 *braciatores* enumerated in 1309 kept open house, but sheer lack of space must have been a limiting factor for many of them. Colin Platt (*The English Medieval Town*, Secker & Warburg 1976) notes that quite generous burgage plots – as much as 60ft wide by 200ft deep – were often provided in new towns to attract settlers. London had no need for such an incentive, though, and its burgage plots – although, naturally enough, no outline of them survives – can hardly have been as large. And even in the new towns both plots and the buildings on them were quickly divided and subdivided as burgesses rented out splinters of desirable town-centre real estate to incomers. Only a handful of medieval townhouses survive in anything like their original dimensions, and none of them in London; what few there are such as those in Lincoln, Bury St Edmunds, Canterbury, and Southampton tend to be at the grander end of the scale and are consequently very spacious. But humbler survivors such as the several rows of 14th-century cottages in York often have a footprint of no more than 17ftx17ft (although the upstairs rooms might be jettied to create a little more floor space). It's hard to imagine a brewer, his family, and their brewery managing to share such cramped quarters with anything more than a very select band of customers.

Nonetheless, having a crew of carousers invade your kitchen was worth the inconvenience because it could make an appreciable difference to the brewery's profitability; for selling for consumption on the premises allowed brewers to circumvent the rules governing both measure and price. A mug of ale could be of any volume, a chopyn being approximately a pint and a gill a half-pint; but neither measure was legally verified. Their very manufacture was prohibited in 1310, but the public burning of an impounded batch in 1370 suggests the ban was less than entirely effective. Alehouse-keepers also habitually kept (or claimed to keep) the first and strongest running of the mash – the best third – back for their on-trade customers, charging what they wanted and blending the two inferior grades for off-trade customers. Once alehouse-keeping became too widespread to suppress, overcharging and short measure became common complaints. As Covetousness boasts in *Piers Plowman*:

"*I boughte hire barly – she brew it to selle.*
Peny ale and puddyng ale she poured togideres
For laborers and lowe folk...

The beste ale lay in my bour or in my bedchambre,
And whoso burned (tasted) therof boughte it therafter –
A galon for a grote (fourpence), God woot, no lesse,
Whan it cam in cuppemele (cupfuls) – this craft my wif used!"

However irregular their retail practices, it seems clear that some brewers were able to establish large and successful on-trade businesses. A brewery in Crooked Lane near London Bridge, owned by Gilbert de Mordone, entered the records on the evening of 25th March 1325 when a 16-strong armed gang tried to kidnap Gilbert's ward Emma. The attempt turned into a street brawl in which the leader of the would-be kidnappers – Walter de Benington, described as a tailor – was killed by a blow to the head; and the incidental details recorded by the coroner tell us some interesting things about a substantial alehouse of the period. For a start, de Mordone's primary occupation was given as "stockfish monger", and as he had the wardship of an heiress worth kidnapping he was presumably a businessman of some substance. (He had also some years previously stood surety for the executors of the will of another merchant who had left two young children – essentially, he was charged with making sure the orphans' guardians didn't embezzle their inheritance). Secondly, he employed a brewer, Geoffrey, who was also caught up in the brawl along with de Mordone's son Robert and a number of neighbours (one of whom struck the fatal blow). Third, the criminals came into the premises and between them drank four gallons of ale in its "*mercatorium*" (yet another word for alehouse!) before embarking on their ill-fated attempt: evidently, then, the *mercatorium* was big enough for at least 16 customers at a time. So here we have a substantial businessman with at least two interests running a brewery with a public bar attached and employing a full-time brewer. One wonders whether de Mordone was selling his ale according to excise, and also whether he had intended to close up before curfew (the incident happened at Compline, the last office of the day before curfew). But these details were of no relevance for the coroner.

The attempted kidnapping of de Mordone's ward is one of only a handful of records from the period of violent crimes occurring in taverns or alehouses – which may come as a surprise, given the modern obsession with attributing all crime to alcohol. In the same coroner's roll that reports the De Mordone case, for instance, we read of the murder of Stephen de Lenne, described as a taverner, by Arcus de Rikelinge, a Brabanter, on 21st December 1323. The two had been playing "*ad tabulas*" (Chess? Backgammon? Shove ha'penny?) in the tavern of William de Standeforde in Dowgate; when de Lenne won, Arcus lured him outside and stabbed him twice in the stomach. But these sensational incidents were rarities. Of more concern to authorities that had the slimmest of resources with which to maintain order in a rapidly-growing city was curfew-breaking or "nightwalking"; and given the necessarily dubious legality of the business model of taverns and alehouses, it was inevitable that they should be caught up in the unending campaign against it.

Edward I Cracks Down

Under the rule of the austere Edward I, who was determined to stamp out the public disorder that seems to have flourished during his father's troubled reign, a series of inquisitions or mass trials sought to make an example of curfew-breakers, with prison sentences that could be commuted for large fines. In four such inquisitions convened by the Mayor, Gregory de Rokesley, in late 1281, a total of 73 men were indicted on a catch-all charge of "divers trespasses, homicides, robberies, and assaults and for being nightwalkers after curfew in the City with swords and bucklers, and for setting up games contrary to the King's peace". The title of these inquisitions – *Inquisitio de nocte vagantibus* – makes it quite clear what offence was being targeted, but frequenting taverns after curfew also figured in the specific charges laid against 11 of the defendants. In six of these cases, the charge was expanded to include playing dice in taverns after curfew.

The link between nightwalkers and their places of resort was recognised in a statute of 1285 asserting that offenders commonly assembled in taverns to plan their crimes and await their opportunities; but oddly omitted from all this were the taverners themselves who, it could be argued, by the simple act of remaining open after curfew were complicit in the various offences committed by their customers. This omission was made good in 1297 in a Mayoral proclamation covering a wide range of topics including street-cleaning and watch-keeping that also forbade taverners or brewers to open after curfew. Another major inquisition in 1311 indicted 38 men for curfew-related offences ranging from assault to fraud, and this time four of the defendants were charged with keeping open house and receiving strangers. They can only have been taverners. Another was charged with enticing people into taverns where gambling was going on – making him a 14th-century schlepper – and a sixth man was described as a taverner but was only charged, rather vaguely, with being a bad character.

Legal attempts to enforce the curfew continued throughout the 14th century, with injunctions of various sorts being made or repeated in 1329, 1353, 1357, 1383 (this time in English rather than the Latin or Norman French hitherto used for legal purposes) and 1393. Often the form of words chosen was the same or virtually the same as in the 1285 statute, suggesting an almost despairing attitude on the part of authorities whose lack of resources rendered them in effect powerless in the face of the citizens' demand for a night-life. After all, if armed men went about at night seeking to assault and rob, there must also have been unarmed and perfectly innocent people going about at night to become their prey; and it is to be presumed that taverners did not remain open after curfew exclusively to feed and water the city's underworld. By the early 15th century the struggle seems to have been abandoned: in 1412 the Lord Mayor ordered taverns to close early on the eves of St John and SS Peter & Paul – early in this case being 10pm. Nevertheless, the continual butting of heads between the city authorities and taverners over the curfew in the 14th century set the tone for relationships between the pub trade and officialdom right down to our own times.

Unfortunately the annalists who made the records did not specify whether these troublesome taverners were retailers of wine or ale: contemporary documents from smaller cities such as Oxford described wine taverns unambiguously as *taberni vinorum*, but in London the unqualified word *taberni* (or *tabernae*) remained the legal generic for any on-trade premises for generations. Before the later 14th century *taberni vinorum* are specified only once in the Letter Books, in a writ to wine assayers of 1310, and Latin never seems to have evolved a separate word for alehouse beyond the *scotallae* that had been used in this sense only once – and early in the preceding century, at that. Only occasionally do the expressions *braciator* and *braceresse* creep into the record in contexts that suggest that they sold for consumption on the premises as well as off.

Later in the century the distinction had become much more obvious: John Gow's *Mirour de l'Omme* (1379), written in Norman French, excoriates the fraudulent *cervoiser* and produces a long list of the tricks by which he defrauds the ale-drinkers – who Gow specifies, even at this late date, are both *anglois* and *povre* – who habitually frequent his *hostel*, spending what little they have. (The choice of the word *hostel* at this time did not imply that the *cervoiser* was also an innkeeper: like the word "inn", to the 14th-century ear it merely meant "house", if perhaps carrying the implication that the house was rather larger and grander than most). Gow's accusations against the publican are, of course, intended as a sermon on social morality rather than an objective description of the contemporary pub trade; but he does reinforce the point that on-sales were one way of effectively dodging the assize. The *cervoiser*, he says "*du malvois blé fait la cervoise malement*" (from poor grain brews ale badly); and if, by chance, he has any ale that is good and pure, then "*le pris en est si halt assise et tant escharce est las mesure qe... la cervoise est pres tant cheris sicomme le vin*". (Its price is assessed so highly and its measure is so short that the ale is almost as dear as wine). Chaucer, too – a Londoner born and bred, son and grandson of vintners, and a close friend of Gow's – makes it clear that by the late 14th century the distinction between tavern and alehouse was well understood: Absolom in *The Miller's Tale* was evidently an inveterate pub-goer for, says the poet, "in al the toun nas brehous ne tavern that he ne visited." By the late 15th century the difference had become explicit for, as a schoolbook of English passages for translation into Latin rather sadly says: "As I hauntede ale howses and wyn taverns, I have spende all the money that I hade in my purse". The imprecision of legal Latin, therefore, need cause no problems for the usual identification of taverns as more upmarket establishments than alehouses: even at the turn of the 13th and 14th centuries the high price of wine – 5-6d a gallon compared to 1½d for a gallon of ale – and the type of custom that wine taverns must therefore have attracted, surely identifies the more disorderly taverns and taverners referred to in the London Letter Books, or City records, from which most of the preceding material is taken, as alehouses and alehouse-keepers rather than wine taverns and vintners.

London's Taverners Go On Strike

But even if the wine taverns were too gentrified to be much troubled by the nightwalkers (commonly indicted as "nightwalkers and bruisers" – *pugnatores*) associated with alehouses, they were not beyond selling short measure, mixing sour wine with sound, and storing red and white wines in the same cellar (a practice thought, in the Middle Ages, to be bad for the health); and the various actions taken against vintners throughout the 14th century and recorded in the Letter Books were more concerned with consumer protection than public order. John Gow, again, rails against the fraudulent practices of wine-merchants. In a long passage in *Mirour de l'Omme*, he outlines the various forms of adulteration and passing-off that the cheating taverner deploys to sell cheap wine at top prices to the "*dames de la Cité*" who "*vienont trotant le petit pas*" to buy wine for their households. Mind you, says Gow, whose moral opprobrium none can escape, the *chambereres* or housewives are in on the act, albeit tacitly, spending rather less of their housekeeping on wine than their husbands intended, and presumably pocketing the difference. But even if they are in effect thieves (*lieres*), the taverner doesn't care so long as he gets his cut.

Gow notwithstanding, taverns and taverners were in fact more strictly regulated than brewers and alehouse-keepers, perhaps because they were frequented by bourgeois consumers who were in a position to insist on their rights. A writ of 1311 required casks of wine to be rested for three days before being broached and to be tasted, approved, and officially marked by the city's assayers, of whom eight or 12 were to be appointed, before going on sale. The same writ banned wholesalers (*grossours*) from retailing either in person or through a third party, as exemplified by the tied lease of 28th May 1284 between Richard de St Botulf, a taverner, and Richard de Hedstrete by which de St Botulf rented a property in Chepe from de Hedstrete for 100s a year and in return undertook to buy from him four casks of wine worth £9 every fortnight. The tied lease was such a convenient device, though, that an ingenious way round the ban was quickly found: in 1319 the aptly-named Thomas Drinkwater built a tavern at Bridge Foot (identified now as the Bear, later to become a famous inn) and leased it to a vintner, James Beaufleur. It turned out that Beaufleur had already paid Drinkwater the "rent", which had paid for the building work; that Drinkwater was actually going to continue running the tavern; and that he would be buying all his wine off Beaufleur. Thus the vintner appeared to be leasing the tavern off the taverner, when in fact it was the other way round – a flagrant defiance of the spirit if not the letter of the 1311 writ.

At the same time the retail price of wine for that year was fixed at 5d a gallon for the best, 4d for the second best, and 3d for the rest. It was a price-cut to 4d for a gallon of Rhenish in 1331 that provoked the taverners to stage a strike and demonstrated how well-organised London trades could be: according to the Letter Books (trans HT

Riley 1868): "And hereupon the said Mayor, Aldermen, and Sheriffs, were given to understand that all the taverners of the City, making a confederacy and alliance among them, had closed the doors of their taverns and would not allow their wines to be sold; in contempt of our Lord the King, and to the annulment of the Ordinances aforesaid, and the common loss of all the people. Upon hearing which, the Mayor and Sheriffs went through the middle of the Vintry and of Chepe, and through other streets and lanes of the City, that they might know the truth as to the same; and they had the names of the taverners so closing their taverns written down, which were as follow: William de Croydone, John Fynche, William le Gaugeour, Robert de Lenne, John Osekyn, Alice atte Laneende, John atte Conduyt, John Blaunche, John Janyn, Agnes Ballard, Alan atte Conduyt, Geoffrey de Bodelee, Richard de Rothinge, John Reynfri, Roger de Thorpe, William de Shirbourne, Edward Cosyn, John de Oxenforde, Alexander de Burgoyne, John Wrothe, Adam de Burgoyne, Thomas Heyroun, Gilbert le Gaugeour, Simon atte Stockes, Richard de Boterwyke, Hugh le Bevere, Richard Sterre, Thomas de Seford, and Ralph Beaufleur.

"And forthwith ... four inquisitions were held, of the best men of the whole city, seeing that there was an immense congregation of citizens there; the first jury being made by John de Bixle, John de Denham, and ten others: who said, upon their oath, that all the taverners of the City, by common assent, had shut the doors of their taverns, and would not allow their wines to be sold... And they said that Hikeman le Taverner of Smethefeld and Reynald de Thorp had sold their wines against the assize made thereon, after the same had been prohibited, secretly within their taverns, their doors being closed, etc."

Unfortunately, the MS breaks off at this point, so we never hear what happened to William de Croydone, John Fynche, William le Gaugeour, Robert de Lenne, John Osekyn, Alice atte Laneende and the rest, nor how their strike was broken (although Hikeman le Taverner of Smethefeld and Reynald de Thorp's clandestine blacklegging can hardly have helped their cause). We do know, though, what became of one of the strikers, Hugh le Bevere: in 1337 he was accused of murdering his wife but, refusing to plead, was imprisoned for life rather than hanged.

Whatever the outcome of the taverners' strike, the authorities' consumer protection campaign went on, with an ordnance forbidding mixing bad wine with good and allowing patrons to inspect tavern cellars in 1337, repeated in 1342 and 1354; another enforcing official inspection of measures in 1352, and so on. The continuous and mechanical promulgation of these writs and ordnances has a hint of official weariness about it; but sometimes the authorities were stirred to action, as John Penrose found in 1364 when he was convicted of selling bad wine and sentenced first to drink some of it and then to stand in the stocks while the rest was poured over his head, and after that to be hauled off to Newgate during his majesty's pleasure. The various regulations were finally collated and codified in 1370, and despite Gow's cheating taverner of the late 1370s, these measures eventually had their effect: a major investigation by the wine assayers in December 1416 revealed that the city's taverners had in stock 278 tuns of red and white wine and 700 half-tuns of sweet wines – an interesting sidelight on contemporary taste – but only four half-tuns of unsound wine.

The sheer volume of court records and legal enactments that survive from the Medieval period make it an even greater shame that we have so little descriptive material relating to alehouses, taverns, and the men and women who ran them and frequented them – other, that is, than the nightwalkers and bruisers. Taverners, we know, could be wealthy – Hugh le Bevere forfeited clothes, household goods, furniture and stock worth more than £15, including two fur robes worth 20s and 16s, when he refused to plead on the charge of murdering his wife; and that excluded his wife's dowry which would have gone back to her family. And taverns could be large: the Peter & Paul in Paternoster Row, built for the sum of £36 in 1342, had a cellar 17ft deep with a garderobe and two fireplaces, ground and first-floor public rooms each with seating for 30; a kitchen and buttery (nothing to do with butter, but a storage-place for butts); and a garrett. Taverns could be extravagantly ornamented, too: in 1375 the mayor and aldermen had to pass an ordinance restricting the length of their signs to 7ft because they obstructed passing horsemen and their weight occasionally pulled down the frontages of the buildings to which they were attached. (The ordinance had to be reissued more or less word for word in 1419, which shows how ineffective medieval enforcement could be!)

Alehouse Customers

But of human portraits of the tavern and alehouse and their habitués, we have only a few; and those few are invariably satirical. The best-known of them undoubtedly is that of Glutton and Beton the Brewster and her crew of merry customers in *Piers Plowman*, from the very end of the 14th century. Langland's censure might have been tinged with more than a little affection for the errant Londoners among whom he lived – he reserved his real fire for their rulers. Read now, it's hard to recognize this episode as a moral tract against drunkenness: it certainly injects a cheery note into Piers's otherwise rather dour world.

On his way to Confession one Friday, Glutton is lured into Beton's alehouse:

Now bigynneth Gloton for to go to shrift,
And kaireth hym to kirkewarde his coupe to shewe.
Ac Beton the Brewestere bad hym good morwe
And asked of hym with that, whiderward he wolde.
"To holy chirche," quod he, "for to here masse,
And sithen I wole be shryven, and synne na moore."
"I have good ale, gossib," quod she, "Gloton, woltow assaye?"

Her simple invitation is quite enough to divert Glutton from his pious purpose, and in he goes. We are left in no doubt that this is a London pub: although a Worcestershire man by origin, Langland eked out a slim living as a chantry priest in Cornhill, and his list of

Glutton's fellow-topers includes many who can only have been Londoners: Hick the hackneyman, Clarice of Cock Lane, a raker of Chepe, Godfrey of Glarlickhithe. It's quite a large establishment, too: Langland lists 24 patrons including Glutton himself. Hick the hackneyman and Clement the Cobbler decide to exchange Clement's cloak for Hick's hood using a method of barter called "new fair": the two items are valued independently by members of the company – the "chapmen ychose this chaffare to preise" – and the owner of the less valuable item makes up the difference. In this case, Clement has to buy Hick a beer.

While all this merriment is going on, Glutton manages to "yglubbe" a gallon and a gill of Beton's ale. Bearing in mind that a medieval pint was generally 12 troy ounces (or 13fl oz avoirdupois), Glutton's intake for the day is only 5½ imperial pints – not a huge amount for a whole day's drinking – but it has such a dramatic effect that Betoun can only have been keeping her strongest ale back for her on-sales customers:

His guttes bigonne to gothelen as two gredy sowes;
He pissed a potel in a Paternoster-while,
And blew his rounde ruwet at his ruggebones ende,
That alle that herde that horn helde hir nose after
And wisshed it hadde ben wexed with a wispe of firses!
He myghte neither steppe ne stonde er he his staf hadde,
And thanne gan he to go like a glemannes bicche
Som tyme aside and som tyme arere,
As whoso leith lynes for to lacche foweles.
And whan he drough to the dore, thanne dymmed hise eighen;
He thrumbled on the thresshold and threw to the erthe.
Clement the Cobelere kaughte hym by the myddel
For to liften hym olofte, and leyde hym on his knowes.
Ac Gloton was a gret cherl and a grym in the liftyng,
And koughed up a cawdel in Clementes lappe.
Is noon so hungry hound in Hertfordshire

Dorste lape of that levynge, so unlovely it smaughte!

Following which he takes to his bed until Sunday. Thus the London pub had not only been born: it had been well and truly christened.

But Beton's lowly and unnamed alehouse with its clientele of working men and working girls is only one aspect of the London pub scene: the anonymous satire *London Lickpenny*, probably composed 20-30 years later, documents the fruitless pursuit of a lawsuit by a luckless – and penniless – Kentish peasant through the labyrinthine and corrupt courts of Westminster, and then takes him out on the street, where he samples – or rather, doesn't sample – the capital's variety of street vendors, cookshops, and taverns.

Then to Westminster gate I went
When the sone was at highe prime.
Cokes to me, they toke good entent,
Called me nere, for to dyne,
And proferyd me good brede, ale, and wyne.
A fayre clothe they began to sprede,
Rybbes of befe, bothe fat and fine;
But for lacke of money I might not spede.

In to London I gan me hy;
Of all the lond it bearethe the prise.
"Hot pescods!" one gan cry,
"Strabery rype, and chery in the ryse!"
One bad me come nere and by some spice;
Pepar and saffron they gan me bede,
Clove, grayns, and flowre of rise.
For lacke of money I might not spede.

Then went I forth by London Stone
Thrwghe-out all Canywike strete.
Drapers to me they called anon;

Grete chepe of clothe, they gan me hete;
Then come there one, and cried "Hot shepes fete!"
"Risshes faire and grene," an othar began to grete;
Both melwell (cod) and makarell I gan mete,
But for lacke of money I myght not spede.

Then I hied me into Estchepe.
One cried, "Ribes of befe, and many a pie!"
Pewtar potts they clatteryd on a heape.
Ther was harpe, pipe and sawtry.
"Ye by Cokke!" "Nay by Cokke!" some began to cry;
Some sange of Jenken and Julian, to get themselves mede.
Full fayne I wold hadd of that mynstralsie,
But for lacke of money I cowld not spede.

Then came the taverner, and toke my by the sleve,
And seyd, "Ser, a pint of wyn would yow assay?"
"Syr," quod I, "it may not greve;
For a peny may do no more then it may."
I dranke a pint, and therefore gan pay;
Sore a-hungred away I yede;
For well London Lykke-peny for ones and eye,
For lake of money I may not spede.

Perhaps a countryman of today might not find London, either in the expense of a voyage through its law-courts or in the astronomical prices charged by its restaurants, so very different!

Finally, there is a mid-15th century satire preserved in a handbook of minstrels's songs, *Songs and Carols*, collected by Thomas Wright and published by the Percy Society in 1847. *I Wyll Tell Yow a Full Good Sport* accompanies a group of housewives who have sneaked out for a drinking session at a tavern (for the full text, see Appendix 3). It's rather an oddity – and completely unlike the brutally misogynistic *Tunning of Eleanour Rumming* of 70 or 80 years later, even though the subject matter is identical – in that the main target of the satire appears to be not so much the truanting women themselves as their husbands, from whom they face a beating if they are found out. Nevertheless, they are determined to make the best of the brief freedom they have snatched.

How sey yow, gossips, is this wyne good?
That it is, quod Elenore, by the rood;
It cherisheth the hart, and comfort the blood;
Such jonckettes among shal mak us lyv long.

Anne, byd fill a pot of muscadell;
fore off all wynes I love it well,
Swete wynes kepe my body in hele;
If I had off it nought, I shuld tak gret thought.

An alternative version exists in which the women are entertained by a harper and dance until "they sette them downe, they myght no more, theyre legges they thought were passyng soore." Perhaps it doesn't tell us as much about the 15th-century tavern as it does about the 15th-century husband, except that this was clearly a much more upmarket bar than Beton's alehouse; that customers brought their own food to be cooked; and that women were not excluded. Perhaps one thing it does tell us, though, is that the 15th-century tavern wasn't so different from the pub of today, except that instead of paying for their drinks as they went the party settled up at the end of the session. And one of them got away with paying less than her fair share, so that hasn't changed either.

CHAPTER 6: TOWN & COUNTRY

The late 13th century saw the climax of an economic boom across Western Europe during which the population of England grew from around 1.5 million at the time of the Conquest to perhaps four million in 1300, with food production soaring and trade increasing vastly.

This was the Medieval Warm Period or Little Climatic Optimum. Lasting from 950 (or so) until 1300 (or thereabouts), it saw prolonged periods of ideal farming weather – of temperate winters and summers with neither flood nor drought, when huge tracts of previously marginal land could be broken to the plough. Much of the potential of the weather's benevolence was lost to phases of destructive warfare: Ethelred the Unready's long struggles with the Danes; William the Conqueror's genocidal harrying of the North; the 20-year civil war between Stephen and Matilda known to contemporaries simply as "The Anarchy", when God and His angels slept. The accession of the Plantagenets in 1154, though, heralded a long period of comparative peace broken only by sporadic tussles between kings and their barons under John, Henry III, and Edward II.

With the end of The Anarchy, the great landowners were able to turn their attention to the arts of peace – and especially, given the expensive and destructive nature of the recent past, to estate management. During the wars, many landowners had let all or part of their demesnes to farmers for a money rent. This had the double advantage of providing them with a liquid income, very desirable in the sudden emergencies and exigencies of war, and of insuring them against damage to their assets, in which event they could still insist on getting their rent. The disadvantage was that the tenant farmers had neither the capital nor the incentive to squeeze the maximum return out of the land, which the various barons, bishops, and abbots now badly needed. Taking, or trying to take, their demesne lands back into direct management and reimposing labour obligations on their tenants instead of cash rents allowed them to maximise their potential revenues and to take advantage of new agricultural practices such as marling. By 1285 interest in estate management had grown to such an extent that the first book on the subject since Roman days, Walter of Henley's *Husbandry*, became that rarest of achievements in medieval publishing – a secular best-seller.

Many landlords started enclosing and cultivating their share of the village commons, often in the face of determined opposition, as well as carving new ploughlands – assarts or, in the north, intakes – out of wasteland and even hunting-grounds. Meanwhile in their northern "deserts", where the population had still not fully recovered from the Conqueror's harrying, the Cistercians were pioneering sheep-ranching, an example that other big landowners were later to follow. Increasing the efficiency and productivity of their agricultural and pastoral concerns was only one way in which great landowners sought to boost their incomes, though.

Fairs and Markets

Although rooted in the land, medieval magnates were well used to exploiting trade as a source of valuable exactions. By the 13th century something like a third of all the grain grown in England was not consumed on the manors where it was produced, but was traded. Population growth saw a commensurate increase in the movement both of necessities such as iron and salt and of higher-value commodities such as wine. The wool trade, which was to make England rich in the later Middle Ages, was just beginning its ascent.

The roads, dreadful as they were, were filling up with traffic, as were the navigable reaches of the country's rivers. With trade comes commerce and with commerce, for the feudal landlord, came the opportunity to extract tolls, rents, and fines from merchants at the locations where they met to do business. And so magnates both lay and religious, and not excluding the King, founded great annual fairs and local weekly markets by the hundred.

The major fairs such as those we have already met at Wey Hill and Stourbridge Common, and the countless lesser ones held throughout the land, undoubtedly represented a great opportunity for brewers and victuallers to make hay while the sun shone. But at the same time they were as much of a hindrance as a help to the emergence of permanent alehouses. For although the merchants who flocked to them were hungry, thirsty, and well-provided with cash, these were one-off events that attracted opportunists who are not otherwise recorded as brewing for sale – such as Matthew the Tanner of Bridge Street, who sold ale at St Ives fair in Huntingdonshire in the late 13th century (Peter Clark, *The English Alehouse*) – and who were in direct competition with the more regular brewers. This free-for-all can have done nothing but obstruct any full-time brewers who might have been inclined to establish permanent and stable victualling businesses; and the fact that the fairs were perforce held out of town meant that they provided little or no custom even for those urban taverns and alehouses that did exist.

St Ives itself, though, might have been the exception. Its week-long Easter Fair, chartered as early as 1110 and held on open land beside a newly-built bridge over the Great Ouse in the Abbot of Ramsey's manor of Slepe, quickly became one of the most important cloth fairs in England. Merchants flocked from all over Northern France and Flanders, and Henry III's wardrobe bought so many of its fine cloths at St Ives that a warehouse had to be built to store them securely. Long before Matthew the Tanner's day a considerable town had sprung up around the fairground: its burgesses made a tidy sum during Easter week by renting out their ground-floor rooms as shops and lock-ups. More important for our purposes, though, is that a weekly market was chartered in 1227; and it seems inconceivable that not one of the brewers of such a flourishing town copied the vintners by encouraging customers to drink (at a premium) on the premises.

And in fact that's exactly what seems to have happened. In 1274, the customary tenants of the neighbouring manor of Houghton-cum-Wyton were jointly charged with going into St Ives to buy their ale at other times than during the fair. On the face of it this implies that one or more of the town brewers had indeed decided to throw open the brewery doors and sell for consumption on the premises, and that the menfolk of the neighbouring village had discovered the simple pleasure of strolling into town for a relaxing pint or two in the pub; or perhaps they had downed tools in some dispute or other and headed off to the alehouse instead. For what other possibilities could there be? The offenders can hardly have been indicted for drinking in St Ives on market day because that would have been perfectly legal, so clearly they weren't in town on business. And it scarcely seems possible that they were shopping for home consumption: the town ale must have been of outstanding quality to be worth lugging the two miles back to the village in the quantities they normally consumed. Anyway, Houghton-cum-Wyton is one of the manors so exhaustively studied by Judith M Bennett; and there was enough brewing going on there at the time to satisfy normal domestic demand without having to import extra supplies from St Ives. Surely the likeliest explanation is that by the late 13th century brewers in the major market centres, and perhaps some of the lesser ones as well, were engaged in some form of on-trade; and whether the men of Houghton-cum-Wyton went into town for pleasure or protest, the important thing is that they went into St Ives; bought ale in an alehouse that was open on days other than market day; and drank it there.

Whatever the now-impenetrable ins and outs of the Houghton-cum-Wyton episode, it does suggest that the chartering of regular markets, often in planned and planted new towns, was a different matter altogether from the creation of great annual fairs. Planted towns in themselves were nothing new: 10th-century Anglo-Saxon kings and earls had founded *burghs* as bulwarks against the Danes, and although many never seem to have progressed beyond their original function as temporary stockades, others developed as markets, administrative hubs, and religious centres: Wimborne Minster in Dorset is a good example of one that succeeded. After the Conquest the invaders also built small towns around their castles, especially in the rebellious west and South Wales, as politically secure headquarters, reservoirs of manpower, and sources of revenue. These towns were not especially numerous – just over 100 were planted between 1100 and 1230 – nor were they especially populous: the vast majority had fewer than 1,000 inhabitants, and 95% of the population were country-dwellers until well after the end of our period. But as the ideal habitat for specialised craftsmen they absorbed more than their share of the local wealth: tanners, dyers, weavers, fullers, wheelwrights, ropemakers, nailers, needlers, saddlers, coopers, even scribes naturally gravitated to towns where their catchment areas were expanded from the confines of their native villages to a trading radius, typically, of 12-15 miles.

These towns – whether organic or, like Winchelsea, King's Lynn, and Ludlow, planted – therefore became both proto-industrial centres and also regular places of exchange for the peasants of surrounding villages; and the magnates who owned them were quick to regulate their activities by chartering weekly or in some cases twice-weekly markets as an orderly way for the peasantry to bring in produce for sale – for which they paid "stallage" to the lord – and to buy what manufactured items they needed. Between 1220 and 1350, according to Colin Platt, more than 1,200 markets were chartered in England and Wales. By the time of the Black Death, for instance, Bedfordshire had 25 markets compared to only three recorded in Domesday.

The 13th-century market town with its settled population, its increasing specialisation of trades, its regular weekly or twice-weekly influx of potential customers, and the flow of cash all these factors generated, ought to have been the perfect milieu for the evolution of alehouses and wine taverns. And indeed we do find records in the 13th century of wine taverns in towns large and important enough to have a good, steady, market for wine: the Rummer in All Saints Lane, Bristol, was a tavern called the Green Lattice in 1241; in Oxford the Mitre in the High Street was a tavern called Croxford's in 1285 when a student riot was recorded there, and the Golden Cross in Cornmarket may have been a tavern run by a man named Mauger a century before that. The Adam & Eve in Bishopsgate, Norwich, claims to have been trading since 1249. These are a handful of the many claims of antiquity which, if not demonstrably spurious, are often hard to establish; but whatever the merit of each individual case, it's not unreasonable to assume that in the most prosperous 13th-century provincial towns the moneyed élite gathered in wine taverns to enjoy each other's company just as better-off Londoners had been doing since the late 11th century.

Alehouses, though, seem to have developed much more slowly even in the larger towns and cities. St Ives may indeed have had an on-trade sufficiently developed to lure the men of Houghton-cum-Wyton by 1274, and we have already alluded to a homicide in a tavern in the Hampshire village of Kelmeston (whose market may not have been large but definitely existed) in 1306; but on the basis of the admittedly scanty documentary evidence these cases seem to have been the exception. Competition from other providers alone must have seriously undermined the viability of full-time alehouses. Many households still brewed their own; board and lodging were often part of the package for servants and apprentices; parish churches and guilds still hosted their own celebrations at which ale was on offer. Market days, of course, were always an opportunity, and there are many records of victuallers and ale-drapers in the bigger market centres setting up temporary booths, just as in Martial's Rome and late Saxon London, to supply visiting shoppers. In Oxford in 1319 these victuallers had to be allocated pitches in designated streets to prevent them from pestering passers-by; but given the absence of regulation it may very well be that many if not most of these opportunistic victuallers were part-timers like Matthew the Tanner.

The main factor inhibiting the evolution of the urban alehouse, though, was the straightforward poverty of most of their potential clientele. The 13th century saw the landowning classes enrich themselves mightily, while a new urban middle class running the gamut from self-employed craftsman to merchant prince was also emerging. Not much of this new prosperity seems to have rubbed off on the workers, however. With the population increasing labour was plentiful and wages fell; and for the same reason basic foodstuffs were in short supply and prices rose. Peasant holdings, too, tended to decrease in size, especially when lords started enclosing parts of the commons. But at least village labourers, even the poorest, actually *had* holdings, so that the rising price of their produce might go some way towards offsetting falling wages. The urban poor, often packed into divided and subdivided tenements in the suburbs, had no such cushion. The aspirational middle classes were natural wine-drinkers. The poorer classes were natural ale-drinkers. Even in the more prosperous later 14th century many of them, according to Langland, had to make do with water; so: not much custom for the putative alehouse keeper there.

Not only were many of the urban ale-drinking classes too poor to be good customers, some of the urban brewers seem to have been just as poor themselves. According to Peter Clark, indigent migrants from the countryside often fell back on their old sideline of brewing for sale as and when necessary, hawking their ale in the streets or from door to door. Competition like this can only have undermined the more regular brewers and deterred them from investing too heavily in their businesses; and by the turn of the 13th-14th centuries there is little unambiguous evidence of urban alehouses in any but the biggest towns such as Oxford where, in 1306, a brawl started in a tavern when a servant of the landlord's tried to take down "the sign of ale" (perhaps to show the pub was closed) and in the ensuing battle one of the University men fled into the cellar "where they sell their ale" (Clark). For the most part, though, the combination of competition and poverty seems to have made the prospect of urban alehouses commercially unviable, and there is little unequivocal evidence to suggest that at the beginning of the 14th century there were many dedicated commercial alehouses challenging home consumption and semi-formal, semi-official organised events as the principal locus of working-class ale-drinking outside London and a handful of other cities.

Then the Medieval Warm Period lurched to an end. From 1301 Europe was dogged by a series of cold winters and wet springs that destroyed harvest after harvest and caused widespread famine; the worst of them, the Great Famine, lasted from 1315 to 1321. According to a contemporary English satire, *Simony and Covetousness*:

For tho God seih that the world was so over gart,
He sente a derthe on eorthe, and made hit ful smarte.
A busshel of whete was at foure shillinges or more,
And so men mihte han i-had a quarter noht yore...
A mannes herte mihte blede for to here the crie
Off pore men that gradden, "Allas, for hunger I die!"

(When God saw that the world was so over proud,
He sent a dearth on earth, and made it full hard.
A bushel of wheat was at four shillings or more,
Of which men might have had a quarter before...
A man's heart might bleed for to hear the cry
Of poor men who called out: 'Alas! For hunger I die!')

And after famine came plague.

Plague and After

The Black Death that arrived on these shores in 1348 was one of those rare historical watersheds, like the Russian Revolution, whose significance is immediately apparent even to contemporaries. Some historians now mark it as the end of the Middle Ages; and indeed for most working-class people at the time the change of dynasty at Bosworth in 1485 that is usually taken as the transition from Medieval to Modern can hardly have made much immediate difference. The enormous economic, social and indeed psychological changes that followed the wiping out of up to a third of the population most certainly did. Yet despite the horrors of 1348-9 and subsequent visitations, the changes were not all bad. The Black Death's immediate and obvious effect was to create a labour shortage, whose immediate and obvious consequence was a rise in wages. Despite the Statute of Labourers of 1351 – a lengthy and rather panicky piece of legislation that tried to hold wages, trade by trade, down to pre-plague levels by force – the labour market was, for once, a seller's market. Peasant purchasing power doubled in the late 14th century and rose by another 50 per cent in the 15th. The economy had already started to swing, despite frequent reactionary backlashes, away from payment of wages, rents, and taxes in kind or labour-service towards payment in cash. After the Black Death, the trend intensified.

But if late 14th-century labourers had more actual cash to spend than their grandparents ever did, they had little to spend it on. The most thrifty took the opportunity to rent holdings left vacant by the plague, founding aspiring dynasties such as the Pastons of Norfolk, yeomen whose descendants became important landholders, whose 15th-century letters survive. The less ambitious could eat better and dress better – which they did – and they could drink more, which they also did. Despite the Black Death's devastation of the population, which didn't recover fully for a century, there is good evidence that ale consumption rose dramatically in the decades that followed. Christopher Dyer's studies of manorial accounts from different parts of England (*Standards of Living in Late Medieval England*, Cambridge University Press 1989, and *Everyday Life in Medieval England*, Hambledon & London 1994) reveal that after the Black Death the proportion of cereals used for brewing and baking shifted in favour of brewing, while the value of ale given to harvest workers in the half-century following the plague was typically 50% greater than in the half-century preceding.

Not only that, but with the coming of war with France imports of wine from Gascony fell by more than half from around five million gallons to around two million, with prices rising from 4-5d to 8d a gallon; and the shortfall was not made up by increased imports from elsewhere. The "squeezed middle", their incomes hit by rising wages and falling rents, were making do with ale instead – and in very considerable quantities: in terms of alcohol content it takes more than six million gallons of mid-strength ale to replace three million gallons of wine.

The comparative prosperity of the post-plague peasantry, grim though the circumstances were, transformed the rural brewing scene and enabled provincial brewers to catch up with their opposite numbers in London and other cities. For despite rising demand, there was dwindling competition. Many of the women who had previously been part-time brewers were, not to put too fine a point on it, dead; and for many of the rest there was now better-paid employment to be had, particularly in the fulling and weaving trades that were migrating from towns to rural areas. Part-time brewing on the traditional pattern did not die out immediately, but the women who chose to stay in the trade had to expand their operations quite dramatically to meet demand. This requirement put the part-timer, especially the single woman, at a grave disadvantage: only those with capital – in effect, those who were married – could afford the outlay on more and bigger vessels and the additional current expenditure on greater quantities of barley and fuel. Married women had yet another advantage: their husbands, as freemen with the right to hold public offices, had clout with the local authorities; and in time it was the husbands who became recognised as the owners of the brewery even if it was still the wives who did the actual brewing.

The result was what we would today call rat-ionalisation: the concentration of brewing in fewer and larger enterprises, along with the appearance of "common" brewers – that is, those who brewed more or less all the time, rather than those who brewed a surplus for sale only occasionally. In London, for example, the 1,334 *braciatores* of the 1309 survey had shrunk to a mere 400 by 1416 (Richard W Unger, *Beer in the Middle Ages and the Renaissance*, University of Pennsylvania Press 2004). There's evidence, too, that this process of contraction was not entirely a natural effect of the workings of the market: the common brewers seem to have conspired in some areas, often with the collusion of the local authorities, to squeeze out the old-fashioned brewsters altogether by organising themselves into rotas so that their products were always available, thereby reducing demand for the sporadic output of their part-time competitors. In Oxford in 1434, for instance, the university permitted just 19 brewers – all men – to brew for sale. (Although the prosecution of a brewster, Alice Everard, five years later for refusing to sell weak ale to the poor indicates that bootlegging is not a modern phenomenon). It's also at this point, quite late in our period, that we can begin to see the fairly widespread emergence, especially in the larger towns, of "tipplers" – not bearing its modern meaning of drinkers, but alehouse keepers who didn't actually brew their own beer but retailed the products of the common brewers. Martyn Cornell notes that as early as 1351 only a third of Oxford's ale-sellers were brewing their own ale; Winchester in 1417 had 36 alehouses that brewed their own and 27 that didn't; and Chester in 1487 had 57 alehouses that brewed and 101 that didn't. Possibly the emergence of non-brewing alehouses was a consequence of the trade of regrator or huckster; tippling as a significant sector in the ale-selling trade, though, really belongs to the 16th and 17th centuries.

Increasing the size of your brewery while watching your competitors fall off one by one was not without its challenges. The Assize of Bread and Ale, though now nearly a century old, was still there to limit your profitability. And since widespread beer-brewing was still some way off – some centuries off, in the more diehard parts of the country – the traditional ale-brewer was still making a perishable product that had to be sold quickly. So while brewing greater quantities presented an opportunity for greater profits, it also carried the risk of greater losses. But the method of speeding up sales and commanding higher prices that had been exploited by your city cousins, previously closed to you by your part-time competitors and by the sheer poverty of most of your customers, was now available, albeit by courtesy of the after-effects of the Black Death. Protected, at least to some extent, by your husband's status in the community, you could ignore the old regulations, dispense your ale in unstamped earthenware chopyns and gills, keep back the first mash to sell at a good premium... and open your kitchen as an alehouse.

This was one of those rare moments in history when all the ducks are in a smart, well-ordered row. For if the brewers of rural and small-town England were now ready to become hostellers and victuallers, their neighbours were ready to become their regular customers. Market days seem already to have assumed something of the character of a day off, and it was in town, on market day, whether at an ale-draper's temporary booth or in a prototypical alehouse, that medieval villagers learned to enjoy a pint for its own sake. Now, and for the first time, many peasants found they had both the time and the money simply to go for a drink when they felt like it. They were all dressed up; and now they had somewhere to go.

Characteristically, the first unambiguous mention we have of small-town brewers exploiting this potential *en masse* comes from the records of a manorial court. In 1369 the market town of Thornbury near Bristol, chartered in 1252, had 20 brewers, every single one of whom was found to be holding back the best-quality third of their output for sale on the premises. "All the brewers of Thornbury, which time they brew, and before the ale-tasters arrive, put aside the third best part of the brew and store it in a lower room. It is sold to no-one outside the house but only by the mug to those frequenting the house as a tavern, the price being at least a penny a quart," said the indictment (Bennett). The transformation of Thornbury's brewers into alehouse keepers was confirmed two years later when one of them, Juliana Fox, was charged with staying open after curfew, running a brothel, and harbouring thieves.

If the erring ale-sellers of Thornbury were the first actually to be recorded as publicans outside London and the bigger boroughs, others were evidently doing the same thing at much the same time. For such were the potential profits of the new habit of drinking on the premises that complaints soon began to abound about brewsters refusing to make off-sales at all. For example, a jury in Wye, Kent, was interrogated in 1371 about brewsters "who are unwilling to sell ale outside their homes in sealed measures, but only to those sitting in their alehouses, who use cups, dishes, and other unreliable measures, and who even sell their ale for 3d a gallon" (Bennett).

Even in the late 1370s, however, a line of Langland's in the C Text of *Piers Plowman* appears to support the idea that alehouses were still a phenomenon of country towns rather than smaller settlements: "eremites that enhabiten the heye weyes and in borwes (boroughs) among brewesters" are his targets on this occasion. But if market towns had been the vector by which the habit of drinking in alehouses had spread from major boroughs and cities to rural market towns, it was another gift of the Black Death's that enhanced the potential viability of alehouses in smaller settlements still.

Passing Trade

The pursuit of higher wages necessarily implied taking to the road, and one result of the plague was that labourers started to do just that. We can't know in what numbers these "peasants out of bond" abandoned their own manors; but they were numerous enough to provoke repeated (and fruitless) attempts to stop them. As late as 1372, more than two decades after the Black Death's first visitation, Parliament was still inveighing against the new-found mobility of the labouring classes, protesting that: "Some flee from one county to another, some go to the great towns and become artificers, some into strange districts to work, on account of the excessive wages, none remaining for certain in any place, whereby the statute (of labourers) cannot be put in execution against them." (quoted by JJ Jusserand, *English Wayfaring Life in the Middle Ages*, 1884). Four years later it was made illegal not only for bonded labourers but also for free men to desert their "*pays propre*"; but as long as the landed class whose own Parliamentary representatives were making such protests and regulations connived in paying illegally high wages to make sure the harvest was got in and the sheep were shorn, the labouring class was happy to accept them. And the landed proprietors, whether they supported the legislation or not, for once had little choice in the matter, for: "as soon as their masters challenge them with bad service, or offer to pay them according to the statute, they flee out of their service and out of their own district... to strange places unknown to their said masters."

The search for better-paid work might not actually take the labourer all that far; and indeed many of the immigrant burgesses of the late 14th century appear to have originated from manors within a radius of no more than 15-20 miles. But permanent migrants to towns can hardly have accounted for all or even a majority of the itinerant farmworkers who so worried the authorities by moving restlessly from manor to manor without apparently intending to settle anywhere. And while trudging the rutted roads they must have needed victualling and, in poor weather, a friendly floor to spend the night on. Peter Clark suggests that they may have relied on friends and relations rather than alehouses to supply these needs, which may have been the case for many of them for some of the time; but they must have represented a degree of potential demand for local alewives and, moreover, a demand of a new kind. To open your kitchen as an alehouse for local trade requires little in the way of commitment; to become a bed and breakfast for wayfarers as well is almost to enter a profession.

Nor were itinerant labourers the only source of demand for the alehouse's hospitality in the post-Black Death countryside. Pedlars or chapmen selling small luxuries – "pynnes, poyntes, laces, gloves, knyves, glasses, tapes or any suche kynde of wares whatsoever" – and tinkers were already familiar visitors; with the general rise in wages after the plague, their goods and services can only have been in more demand; and now they had not only a place to sleep when the weather was too rough for camping out, but also a congenial place to do business where a pot of ale might help to sway the hesitant purchaser. Combined with the reduction in the number of women brewing for sale and the comparative prosperity of the peasant workforce, this incremental increase in demand can only have made alehouse-keeping an even more attractive proposition.

The law still forbade this new style of retailing, but local courts soon gave up trying to enforce it. Manorial courts, after all, were composed of local villagers and townsfolk who enjoyed the new habit of drinking on the premises as much as their neighbours did. And even those jurors who preferred the old ways had to consider their neighbours' opinion and think twice before cracking down on an innovation that seems to have been widely appreciated. Not only that, but now that the profession of brewer-hosteller was, on paper at least, safely in male hands it was becoming both a substantial and a respectable one, and alehouse keepers frequently had other business interests – just like Gilbert de Mordone, who we met in London in

1325 – that made them even more substantial and respectable. The Cock in Gamlingay, Cambridgeshire, first attested in a deed of 1445 (James Brown, *Villagers: 750 Years of Life in an English Village*, Amberley Publishing 2011), was also a considerable farm whose toft, until the far end was built on in the 1970s, stretched back some 400 yards from the street; while in the last decade of the 14th century in Stockton, Wiltshire, the village's most prolific brewer, John Warner, also described himself as a baker, hosteller, and victualler (Bennett). In the late 14th and early 15th centuries, therefore, not only do we find presentments under the old Assize becoming more and more infrequent, but many courts did away with its legal fictions completely and replaced the "fines" with a straightforward annual fee, the tolcester. Rowland Parker's study of the Cambridgeshire village of Foxton, *The Common Stream* (William Collins, 1975), records the manorial court still trying in vain to enforce the assize well into the reign of Henry VIII, but none of the brewers presented appears to have paid their fines; and the whole structure of price-control was finally blown away by the hyper-inflation of the 1540s.

Nevertheless, the old ways of village life took a long time to die out. Throughout the 15th century and into the 16th the Church still hosted bid ales and scot ales, increasingly held not in the parish church itself but in "church houses" or parish halls, some of which survive today as pubs and many of which, according to local tradition, were originally built as hostels for itinerant masons working on the parish churches themselves. The same church houses still witnessed the communal feasts that marked the great days of the liturgical calendar. Religious guilds still held feasts of their own. Landowners still treated their labourers to free food and ale, although less regularly than before. But despite the continuing sources of competition, alehouses proliferated in the country towns and villages of 15th-century England – and, indeed, of 15th-century Wales.

Trouble Brewing

Where there is alcohol, trouble is never very far away. On 14 January 1402 Guy, Bishop of St David's, wrote to the Abbot of St Dogmael's in Ceredigion following his visitations to the sadly-decayed Abbey (which had only four monks): "Whereas we by our ordinary authority making a visitation ... found that from the excessive wandering of the lay brothers among secular persons and dishonourable frequenting of unlawful places, to wit taverns, very great evils and scandals have resulted to the same monastery, we enjoin on you that none of you go to the said town of St Dogmells into any tavern, nor make drinking bouts with anyone outside the bounds (nor also at Cardigan), except it be for some honest matter and for a cause which can be approved of... Also we enjoin that brother Howel Lange, on account of his excess and the evil deeds committed by him, shall not drink wine nor metheglin, on which it has been his habit to get drunk, but he shall give away and distribute his portion to the poor in the abbot's presence; and in this year he shall not go out of the bounds of the monastery unless in the abbot's company. Also we enjoin on the said monks and lay brothers that none of them shall go out of the bounds of the monastery without the special license of the abbot or in his absence of his deputy, and that such licence shall not be too liberal or too continuous. Also that no women suspected in regard to the monks shall lodge in the town but they shall be removed altogether..." (trans Glen Johnson, www.glen-johnson.co.uk).

Bibulous monks are perhaps the stuff of comedy; but just as in the reign of Edward I and his *Inquisitio de nocte vagantibus*, more serious disorder was also associated with alehouses. Peter Clark cites a petition from Norfolk dated 1454 seeking the suppression of a gang of rioters armed with bows, "shooting and playing in men's closes among men's cattle, going from alehouse to alehouse and menacing such as they hated". More problematic for the authorities than men with bows, though, were men without bows. Pastimes such as football, bowls, cock-fighting and "cambuca" or golf were often accused of luring men away from their obligatory archery practice, and Edward III, Richard II, and Edward IV all made pronouncements on the subject. Edward IV's is most explicit, ordering every town and village to provide butts, every able-bodied man (whether English or Irish) to possess a bow his own height, and every feast-day to be spent at least partly in archery practice. Alehouses are not actually cited in the various pieces of legislation as being responsible for luring men away from the butts; but James Brown found, in the Gamlingay court rolls for 1475, that "William Gosson, innkeeper, aided by various people, played unlawful games and sports, namely football, tennis, and tables (backgammon?) on feast days and at other illegal times", for which he was fined 6d. However it wasn't until the very end of our period that a specific connection between the lure of the alehouse and absence from the butts was made at the highest level. By an Act of 1495 Henry VII empowered the local Justices of the Peace to close any alehouse where gaming and disorder were rife or which kept villagers from their bows and arrows. It wasn't quite the first Licensing Act – that came half a century later, in 1552 – but it is the prototype; and its very necessity is a firm indicator that, at last, the alehouse had become not only more or less ubiquitous – Rowland Parker found four of them operating in Foxton at the end of the 15th century – but were also a transformative influence in the lives of the country's 8,000 villages.

And indeed one can't help wondering just how powerful a transformative influence the local alehouse was. If it was really responsible for the widespread neglect of archery practice, that in itself was significant enough: it takes years of practice to make an efficient archer, while a musketeer can be trained in a few months. The early firearm was a hideously inefficient weapon compared to the longbow; but if the battle-ready bowmen weren't available because their local alehouses had lured them away from their training, then army commanders would have to make do with arquebusiers instead. So perhaps we owe modern warfare to the late medieval alehouses of England? And perhaps we owe it more than that.

Medieval England had a long tradition of satirical balladry, culminating with Chaucer and Langland but stretching back two centuries before then. *Simony and Covetousness*, quoted above, is just one example of dozens that are extant, and their common theme is clerical and lordly greed and the injustice and oppression suffered by the poor. The Black Death may have made the villeins less poor, but it didn't make them any less indignant – rather the reverse. Revolutions rarely spring from the most deprived sections of society: more often they are fomented and organised by people of middle rank who feel the system is cheating them of the opportunity to rise yet further. Marx, Lenin, Castro, Mao – these were not the offspring of poor families, but people who learnt their discontent from their bourgeois backgrounds. Robin Hood, in the earliest of the deeply subversive ballads, was first imagined as just such a person: neither poor peasant nor dispossessed aristocrat (a 16th-century interpolation intended to neutralise his subversive potential), but a yeoman – a skilled worker and economically a cut above the peasant, but still deprived of the full fruits of his status by the rigid social hierarchy of the times. In the aftermath of the Black Death many members of the upper strata of village life must have felt the same frustration at a system which defined them as villeins – the property, in effect, of their landlords, with no credible aspiration ever to be more. The leader of the Peasants' Revolt of 1381 bore the surname Tyler: a newly-affluent craftsman in a seller's market, yet still a villein. But now for the first time such people had a neutral arena, the alehouse – a plastic, informal, social space without any imposed structure or agenda, and without any official supervision – where they could meet, grumble, embolden each other, and finally dare to plot.

Did the spreading network of alehouses provide nodal points where wandering malcontents, like the radical preacher John Ball, could spread the message of defiance from village to village? Slightly after the end of our period, in 1545, Henry VIII recognised the subversive potential of the pub when he told Parliament that the Bible, newly available to common people, was "disputed, rhymed, sung and jangled in every alehouse and tavern" in the land (quoted by ST Bindoff, *Tudor England*, Pelican 1950). So it might go beyond the evidence, but not beyond credibility, to suggest that the working class's six-century war of emancipation was declared in a pub

CHAPTER 7: THE OLDEST INN IN ENGLAND

Which is the oldest pub in England? It's a question often asked, and a title often claimed. There are a dozen or so contenders; and apart from those two ludicrous imposters the Fighting Cocks in St Albans, which is no older than 16th century, and the Trip to Jerusalem in Nottingham, which is 200 years younger than that but may stand on the foundations of the Castle's medieval brewhouse, they are all inns rather than alehouses or taverns.

The distinction is important. The word "inn" originally meant no more and no less than a place to stay, and in the Middle Ages that's all inns were. The inn and the alehouse were as different as a Travelodge and a Wetherspoon. Towards the end of our period, when alehouses were already beginning to establish themselves across the country, some innkeepers started selling ale to all comers rather than restricting themselves to serving travellers; but before then inns were an inhibiting factor in the development of the alehouse, selling their own ale and soaking up the passing trade in direct competition with local brewsters.

Wayside Inns

Given the notoriously poor condition of Medieval England's roads, it's surprising to discover how busy they were. For those who hold the traditional view of English medieval history, this poses a problem. It was always taught in schools that the bulk of the population, 95 per cent or more, were subsistence farmers whose lives were, in a sense, sedentary. And yes, 95 per cent or more lived in the country rather than the town, but that didn't make them sedentary – or not all of them anyway. England's roads and towns are studded with inns that are undeniably medieval, and many more have been lost over the years. So who was doing the travelling?

In fact medieval society was not as static as was once taught. Kings and their courts travelled ceaselessly, consuming the produce of royal manors and forests, holding Parliaments, doing justice, cowing the mighty, showing themselves to the people and, as often as not, campaigning. We know from Geoffrey of Monmouth how far and fast the restless Henry II ranged, and how hard it was for a court constantly on the move to function. Barons and prelates great and middling lived in much the same way, particularly those with manors in different parts of the country; and particularly in the earlier part of the period when in order to enjoy the produce of your manors you physically had to visit them. Warfare, too, generated travellers, and not just in the form of armies on the march. Levies from scattered baronial estates often had to travel long distances from their villages to the muster, as did conscripts from towns summoned by commission of array.

Merchants based in the major ports made the rounds of the great fairs, buying and selling wool and finished cloth as well as wine, spices, and other luxuries. They fed into a network of local dealers from substantial wholesalers down to peddlers in trinkets, who also travelled substantial distances. And there was a widespread trade in less glamorous commodities, too. The country would have starved in winter without salt, for instance, and most of it had to be carried over long distances from Cheshire and Worcestershire. Iron was another essential that had to be traded all over the country from a handful of mining areas. Livestock travelled along a network of drove roads, many of them now lost. The movement of these bulk goods involved large numbers of men who all had to be lodged and victualled, however primitively.

The rutted roads of Merrie Englande, then, were if not quite seething certainly not deserted; and while the lesser peripatetics might commonly sleep in a barn or under a hedge, or even on the floor of a wayside alehouse, many of the travellers preferred and could afford the (purely comparative) comfort of an inn.

The first post-Conquest inns were not commercial enterprises as we know them. In most villages, travellers could put up at the only public building apart from the church: the manor-house. The lord and lady may have had their own chamber, but the rest of the household ate and slept together in the hall; a traveller or two can hardly have put much strain on resources. Probably they were welcome, for they brought news and must also tip the steward and servants of the household. As a rhyme from 12th-century Norfolk, quoted by Peter Clark, records:

"In a village there may be
Men of some nobility:
Five or six or even more,
Who keep a hospitable door;
For a guest it is but meet
To offer bread that's made of wheat."

And as barons built themselves new and more comfortable homes, they often let their old homes as inns: one example is the Spread Eagle at Midhurst, Sussex, a manor of the de Bohuns until they became earls of Hereford and upgraded to grander quarters.

But most if not all of England's oldest inns were monastic foundations, built in obedience to the charitable duty of hospitality. Every abbey, convent, and priory had its *hospitium* or hostel for common travellers, while more elevated guests might put up in the Abbot's own lodging. The cost to a monastery of providing for guests or *supervenientes* could be considerable: the accounts of the Knights Hospitallers' Priory at Clerkenwell record a loss of £22.11.4d for

1338 "caused by the hospitality offered to strangers, members of the royal family, and to other grandees of the realm who stay at Clerkenwell and remain there at the cost of the house" (Jusserand). The nobles who thought they had a right to outstay their welcome in this way had some justice on their sides: it was they and their forbears, after all, who had endowed these very abbeys in the first place. Nevertheless the burden of hospitality weighed heavy on well-located religious houses such as Clerkenwell, especially as great magnates travelled with large and demanding retinues who had to be put up in the *hospitium*. Richard de Swinfield, Bishop of Hereford (1282-1317), had a household of 40, most of whom accompanied him on his tours of visitation; and Clerkenwell's sister-house at Hampton complained piteously of the numbers it was expected to feed and shelter owing to the proximity of the home of the Duke of Cornwall. Edward I by a Statute of 1280 tried vainly to limit the right of free hospitality to the deserving poor, formally invited guests, and the actual founder of the house in question: Edward II not once but twice – in 1309 and 1316 – had to confirm the Statute and pledge that neither he nor his household would break it. At the same time, commissions of enquiry were interrogating local people about abuse of monastic hospitality by the gentry, and asking whether intimidation was ever involved.

Clerkenwell's bright red debit column, 22 years after the second restatement of Edward I's statute, demonstrates the futility of all such measures (and as late as 1377 monastery almoners were still complaining that the sheriffs with their retinues, wives, and children, installed themselves in *hospitia* while on official business without making a contribution) and will lead us, in due course, to Harry Bailey of Chaucer's Tabard. For it is thanks to Chaucer that the class of traveller who dominates our image of life on the road in the Middle Ages, whether genuinely representative or not, is the pilgrim.

Pilgrims' Inns

Pilgrimage had both eternal and secular benefits. Prayers at the shrine of a martyr brought not only grace, but also healing. It was for many the only chance of a break from the harsh routine of subsistence farming; and to a serf tied to the land it even offered a chance of freedom. In theory, the lord could not stop his serfs going on pilgrimage, and if they managed to stay away from the manor for a year and a day, they were free. The best-known shrines in England, and the only ones able to draw foreigners in any number, were the tomb of St Thomas Becket at Canterbury and the scene of Richelda de Faverche's vision of Our Lady at Walsingham. But there were, if not hundreds, certainly dozens of other places of pilgrimage across England: Westminster had the tomb of Edward the Confessor; Glastonbury had the thorn tree of Joseph of Arimathaea; Gloucester had the tomb of Edward II; Norwich, York, Lincoln, Hereford, Oxford and many lesser places also had relics with the power to draw pilgrims. But Canterbury was the greatest of them all, England's Compostella or Tours; and the Pilgrims' Way, linking the city with the interior of the country and the south coast ports, was certainly the most important route of pilgrimage. It started properly at Winchester, where groups of pilgrims from the West Country, the Midlands and Wales, along with foreigners who disembarked at Southampton, joined up for a journey of over 100 miles via Farnham, Guildford, West Malling, Aylesford, Maidstone and Charing.

Along this route were many *hospitia* provided mainly by monasteries but also by civic authorities and religious guilds to receive footsore pilgrims – free of charge, but donations always welcome. In Winchester itself, poor pilgrims could shelter at the hospitals of St Cross and St John or at the Hundred Men's Hall. At Farnham there was Waverley Abbey, and at Guildford the Black Friars' hospice. Then there was St Mary's Abbey at West Malling; the Whitefriars' Pilgrims' Hall at Aylesford; Bishop Boniface's Hospital at Maidstone; and in Canterbury itself two abbeys, two friaries and two hospitals.

All of these were free, decent, and clean; and doubtless the accommodation and food were more than adequate for the poorer sort. But as we have seen, economic progress created an increasingly affluent middle class who wanted something better and could afford to pay for it; and from a fairly early period commercial inns began to emerge to meet the demand. Why sleep with the hoi-polloi on the rushes in a cheerless dormitory when for 4d you could enjoy a warmer fire, livelier company, and something more satisfying in the way of victuals at such inns as the Godbegot at Winchester, the Bush at Farnham, the Angel at Guildford, the White Hart at Bletchingly, the Crown or the Old Bell at Oxted, and the Chequers, the White Hart (now the Falstaff) or the Sun in Canterbury itself?

All these inns had one thing in common: they had started life as straightforward *hospitia* but had been leased to or perhaps managed by secular operators and were run for a profit. The best-known example of a businessman running an inn owned by a religious institution is none other than Harry Bailey, Chaucer's host of the Tabard in Southwark. The Tabard was built in about 1305 as the London residence of the Abbot of Hyde. In the subsidy rolls of 1380-81 Bailey is listed as the hosteller; but as he represented Southwark in the Parliaments 1376 and 1378 he may have been at the helm of the Tabard for some time before that. In 1381 he served as the local collector of the infamous Poll Tax, confirming the impression that the Tabard was a substantial enterprise and its host was an important man in the community. And perhaps it was the commercial potential of inns like the Tabard that sparked the golden age of the monastic hospices in the late 14th and 15th centuries, when many of the country's finest inns were built. (Although there exists a petition of 1402 from the House of Commons protesting that corrupt clergy were allowing their guest-houses to fall into decay, which may have acted as an additional spur to their refurbishment or complete replacement).

Perhaps two dozen, possibly a few more, of these inns survive and still trade in something like their original shapes (external shapes, that is: you would be very surprised to walk through the door of some ancient inn and find that inside, it was still an ancient inn!); very many more were rebuilt in the Tudor and Georgian periods and, although barely recognisable, at least occupy the plots where late Medieval *hospitia* once stood. This is perhaps not the occasion for a gazetteer of the survivors; and anyway, most of them are already well-known to everyone with even a passing interest in the subject. But among the most architecturally complete are representatives of three very different types of inn: the Angel & Royal at Grantham in Lincolnshire, the George at Norton St Philip in Somerset, and the New Inn in Gloucester.

Oldest of our trio is the Angel & Royal, a Georgianised but still recognisably gothic gatehouse type fronting the old Great North Road. Originally a *hospitium* of the Knights Templar, its location guaranteed it a steady stream of very important *subvenientes* including (reputedly) King John in 1213. On the suppression of the Templars in 1308 it was confiscated and granted, like a lot of property in the district, to the Hospitallers. It was rebuilt in the reign of Edward III (1327-77), although the only work visible from that period is the gate itself: Edward's bust and that of his queen, Philippa of Hainault, adorn the ends of its hood moulding. The ashlar facade, sash windows, central oriel, bays, buttresses and tracery parapet are all later additions; but inside you can still see 14th-century fireplaces and vaulted stone ceilings, as well as the preserved *Chambre du Roi* where Richard III wrote to his chamberlain sending for his Great Seal so that he could endorse the death warrants of the Duke of Buckingham and other rebels in October 1483. The Angel is known as a gatehouse type because it occupies the whole frontage of a deep and fairly broad burgage plot, allowing a symmetrical design with a central gateway like a castle gatehouse. At the back, a long range of Georgian stables with hotel rooms above has replaced the original medieval stabling.

The George at Norton St Philip in Somerset looks far more ancient, perhaps because it was left alone by the Georgians during the coaching era. In fact it was founded in 1397 by the monks of Hinton Charterhouse principally as a warehouse and exchange for their wool, but also as a guest-house for the merchants who bought it and any other travellers who might happen by, including pilgrims on their way to and from Glastonbury. A stone stair running up a platform in front of the slightly elevated main door furnished a loading bay for wagons, while a great hall on the first floor served as the wool exchange. Originally the George was all of stone, but the half-timbered upper floors date from the aftermath of a fire in about 1500. This gives the front an informality which contrasts strongly with the rear, where a stone stair-turret and mullioned trefoil windows are relics of the more disciplined ecclesiastic architecture of the original. The George's tiny yard – in stark contrast with the expansive plot behind the Angel & Royal – also boasts a gallery, albeit a very short one, which is perhaps the earliest surviving example of a plan which became the standard on cramped town-centre (or, in the George's case, village-centre) sites for three centuries.

A much grander galleried courtyard is to be found at the magnificent New Inn in Northgate Street, Gloucester, built by the Abbey of St Peter in 1445 to accommodate pilgrims visiting the tomb of the murdered Edward II in the cathedral. As with the George, the design is predicated by the cramped nature of the site, but here the galleries surround the courtyard and rise to two stories. The upper tier was enclosed in Georgian times, but on the lower level the bedroom doors still open directly on to the gallery. The stabling was in a second courtyard at the back of the site. Although the facades have been altered and added to over the centuries, the plan and much of the decorative detail are original.

It used to be argued that the Crusaders brought the idea of the galleried courtyard back with them from the East, in imitation of the colonnaded pleasure-gardens of their enemies. If this were so, then the Saracens may have copied it from the Byzantines, who in turn inherited it from Rome – which would make the New Inn at Gloucester a distant cousin of the villa at Fishbourne in Sussex, whose remains are clearly grouped round a peristyle, or courtyard-garden. It's not a theory that has stood the test of time. The courtyard plan is most common in urban settings where it is, quite simply, the only practical way of making the most of the typical long, narrow burgage plot. The gallery, meanwhile, is the most economical way of expanding in the only possible direction – upwards. And the galleried design met the demand for a luxurious innovation: the private room. Had you arrived at a *hospitium* in the 13th or even the early 14th century, you would have eaten with the rest of the guests round trestle tables in the great hall. At night, when the trestles had been stacked away, you would have curled up to sleep in your cloak, perhaps on a straw mattress, but quite likely on the rushes strewn on the floor. But sleeping on rushes that probably contained fleas and lice, rats and mice, scraps of food, spilt ale, and quite possibly dog-droppings was only acceptable when nothing better was to be had: once inns had begun to offer private chambers to the well-to-do – and especially to merchants with stock and specie to keep under lock and key – every other traveller aspired to one too.

But travelling in style was expensive. Thorold Rogers, in his *History of Agriculture & Prices* (1866), quoted by Jusserand, records the costs incurred by the Warden of Merton College, two fellows, and four servants on a journey from Oxford to Durham in the winter of 1331. Given that the cost of their firing is itemised separately, it appears that the party normally shared a single room for which, on one particular Sunday, they paid 2d. For fuel and candles they paid 2¼d, for bread, meat, and pottage 5¾d, for ale and wine 3¼d, and for fodder for their horses the large sum of 10d – a farthing short of two shillings all told, and considerably more than a week's wages for a labourer. On another occasion they spent 18d on a fresh salmon and another 8d to have it dressed and cooked. Condiments such as pickle and gravy would cost them a halfpenny while a screw of sugar cost an astronomical 4d. Prices were always a preoccupation of the authorities, but never more so than immediately after the Black Death, and in 1350 Edward III promulgated a Statute requiring "hostellers et herbergers" to sell food at reasonable prices. The Statute was re-enacted only four years later with a resounding condemnation of the "great and outrageous cost of victuals kept up by innkeepers to the great detriment of the people travelling across the realm", which was perhaps a response to the inflation caused by the plague's shocking mortality rate.

Other than Edward III's futile measures against price inflation, however, and perhaps because of their connections with religious houses, inns up and down the country seem to have been lightly regulated by the standard of the times. It's not even certain that they were bound by the Assize of Bread & Ale, for they were rarely if ever presented for infringements. The same cannot be said of inns and innkeepers in London.

The Inns of London

Medieval London was constantly expanding and was destined to become the biggest city and the busiest port in Christendom, if not the world. The constant coming and going of merchants, of litigants, of diplomats, and of nobles and leading clerics created a transient population whose numbers cannot even be guessed at, with a commensurate demand for accommodation from an early date. As early as the fire regulations of 1212 we hear of bakers and cookshops being forbidden to run boarding-houses (in 1358, the tables were turned when hostellers were forbidden to bake!); and the terms "hosteller" and "herbergour" had first been recorded in 1184 and 1204 respectively (Pete Brown, *Shakespeare's Local*, Macmillan 2012). But the genesis of the capital's inns – and there were many – cannot have been in humble boarding houses above bakeries and cookshops. Many of the transients were wealthy and influential; many others were at least moderately affluent and had certain expectations. Where did they stay when in town?

As we have seen, space was at a premium in a crowded city where plots and tenements were routinely divided and subdivided. Trade guilds and foreign merchants had their halls, but in general the only premises of a size suitable for use as inns were the *hospitia* of religious institutions and the townhouses of lay magnates. In the 14th century, as Westminster became more and more the national focus of law, politics, and diplomacy, the southern side of the river and the no man's land between Whitehall and Ludgate soon became packed with them. Southwark was home to the London palaces of many leading prelates – Lambeth Palace is still with us, and the Bishop of Winchester's compound became notorious for his prison, the Clink, and for the "stews", which were London's principal red light district until suppressed by Henry VIII. These large religious establishments included buildings that proved suitable for conversion into commercial inns: the Abbot of Hyde's London residence, as we have seen, became the immortal Tabard; and one of the Inns of Chancery, New Inn on the Strand, had been Our Lady's Inn – strongly implying a religious origin – before it was taken over as a law school in the 14th century.

Lay magnates also owned many such suitable premises. How great and grand some of them were is shown by the antiquarian John Stow's description of Warwick the Kingmaker's House in Warwick Lane in the City itself: "Richard Neuell Earle of Warwicke, with 600 men all in red Jackets imbrodered with ragged staues before and behind, was lodged in Warwicke Lane: in whose house there was oftentimes six oxen eaten at a breakfast, and ... he that had any acquaintance in that house might have there so much of sodden and rost meate as hee could pricke and carrie vpon a long dagger." Warwick's house, and John of Gaunt's Savoy Palace in the Strand, were doubtless the biggest of such establishments; but there were many other lesser houses where an ambitious aristocrat could dispense largesse and favours just as he did in the great hall of his ancestral castle. The proprietor himself might only be in residence when he had business in town; but during his absence his steward and servants kept open doors just as much in his presence and so, insensibly, his "inn" (for this is the origin of the word) became… an inn. And when great families either moved to better quarters or died out altogether, their former inns continued to receive guests, but under new management. The Paston Letters provide one such example. When the hero of the Hundred Years' War, Sir John Fastolfe, died without heir in November 1459 he left almost his entire estate to his protégé and neighbour, the Norfolk squire John Paston. Henry Windsor, the steward of Fastolfe's house in Southwark – which was already operating as an inn called the Boar's Head, perhaps since Fastolfe's retirement in 1454 to his newly-built castle at Caister – promptly wrote to Paston reminding him that he had been promised the position of hosteller. Paston's reply has not survived, but the Boar's Head did: it only closed in 1720 and its last remnants were demolished in 1830. John Stow in his late 16th-century *Survey of London* mentions two more such cases, both within the City itself. In Lombard Street: "is a common osterie for trauellers called the George… said to haue perteyned to the Earle Ferrers, and was his London lodging," while in Fish Street Hill: "is one great house, for the most part builded of stone, which pertained sometime to Edward the Black Prince, who was in his lifetime lodged there. It is now altered to a common hosterie, hauing the blacke bell for a signe."

The nine Inns of Chancery (which were subservient to the four Inns of Court) were founded in the late 13th century when legal training moved out of London proper to be closer to Westminster. At least one, as we have seen, seems to have had a religious origin. Of the others, Clifford's and Furnival had originally been the London townhouses of the eponymous noble families; Lyons was said to have been already ancient when the students moved in; and Staple's (still to be seen in Holborn, opposite the end of Gray's Inn Road) had previously been favoured by visiting wool merchants. That their founders were able simply to acquire existing hostelries and fill them with law students instead of travelling businessmen shows that by this time London already had a stock of inns that could be bought and sold.

But something about inns – and, more part-icularly, innkeepers – puzzled the authorities. Perhaps because many of them were effectively the household servants of feudal magnates they counted as "foreigners", who shouldn't by rights be trading in London at all. If you were a fishmonger or a cordwainer or a vintner or any other recognised trade you had to be a member of a guild and a freeman of the city; but was innkeeping even a trade? These people stood outside the established order which – given the curiously Orwellian mindset that seems to pervade Medieval legal thinking – meant that *ipso facto* they must be disorderly. In the 1280s, when he wasn't too busy subduing the Welsh, Edward I turned his attention to the problems of law and order besetting a city whose growth was outstripping its administrative resources. We have already encountered his *Inquisitio de nocte vagantibus* of 1281 and its legal onslaught on "nightwalkers" and the taverns they frequented after curfew. In 1285, amid the plethora of legislation contained in the Westminster and Winchester Statutes, we find the surely exaggerated complaint that "divers persons do resort unto the city... of these some do become... hostellers and innkeepers ... as freely as though they were good and lawful men of the franchise of the city ... and some do nothing but run up and down through the streets, more by night than by day, and are well-attired in clothing and array and have their foods of delicate meat and costly; neither do they use any craft or merchandise, nor have they any lands or tenements whereof to live, nor any friends to find them, and through such persons many perils do happen." It may be hard to imagine that innkeepers as a profession were any more prone to doing nothing but running up and down through the streets more by night than by day than any other; but this characterisation provided the necessary moral foundation for the authorities' campaign to bring hostellers into the fold of recognised and regulated freemen.

Two measures enacted between 1285 and 1299, when Edward suspended London's Mayor and Corporation and ran the city through royally-appointed governors, were intended to make innkeepers respectable and remind them of their duty in helping to maintain the King's Peace. One was to insist that hostellers, like other tradesmen, should be freemen of the city: "No foreigner nor stranger to keep hostel within the City, but only those who are freemen of the City, or who can produce a good character from the place whence they have come, and are ready to find sureties for good behaviour. And if any hosteller be found, in contravention of these ordinances, after one month from the date of publication of the same, they are to be arrested and punished." Another, to be frequently repeated and elaborated, made innkeepers responsible for the behaviour of their guests: "Also that no one take another into his house for more than one night, unless he hold him to right if he make default, and his host answer for him if he departs." In 1354 it was further specified: "that hostellers warn their guests to lay aside their arms on entering their hostels." They were also put under oath to "labour as far as ye may to be privy and oversee all manner of merchandise that any alien merchant being under your said hostage and oversight has and shall have coming here after into his possession."

With these enactments, innkeeping officially became a respectable trade. Individual innkeepers like Harry Bailey were made available for public service, as every good freeman ought to be; and innkeepers as a corporation could defend their interests as in 1327, when they collaborated with the haymongers to petition against "foreigners" bringing hay in on the Thames to sell from private houses (the 1358 prohibition on innkeepers baking being a reminder that monopolies can cut both ways). In 1446 the trade was prestigious enough to found its own guild, the Mistery of Hostellers, changed in 1473 to the Guild of Innholders as the status of hosteller started its slide down the social scale to that of "ostler", or mere groom. It was granted its charter as the Worshipful Company of Innholders in 1514.

Nearly half of London's inns were denied the privilege of guild membership, though, since they were not technically in London. A census or register of inns taken in 1384 and not including Southwark, cited by Pete Brown in *Shakespeare's Local,* counted 197 of them, of which 95 were outside the city boundaries in Faringdon, Holborn, Fleet Street, and Smithfield. Brown suggests that this may have been because innkeepers wanted to escape being stifled by city regulations; but as we have seen, regulation cuts both ways, and there are two likelier explanations for this pattern of distribution. We have already touched on the question of size; and to innkeepers, size mattered. Beton the Brewster of Piers Plowman had 24 customers in her alehouse on the day of Glutton's embarrassment; Gilbert de Mordone had at least 16 in his on the day of the kidnap attempt in 1325. To seat 24 or even 16 drinkers at a time requires more space than an ordinary-sized tenement kitchen would provide; to put them up for the night, feed them, and stable their horses as well requires more still. The older inns taken over to become Inns of Chancery each had room for more than 100 students, and it's no accident that they are all just outside the old city walls, for there can have been few such capacious sites inside the cramped and crowded city itself. The other question is one of location. The district between Westminster (politics, diplomacy, and law) and the City (business and commerce) are equally handy for both – hence the concentration of inns in Faringdon and the Strand. Brown also cites the 22 inns recorded in Southwark for the 1381 Poll Tax; but then as Southwark's high street crossed London Bridge, it was the only means of access to the city from the Channel ports and hence just where one would expect to find inns.

Distinctions Begin to Blur

By 1400, then, London and its suburbs had more than 200 inns and the country as a whole had possibly 1,000-1,500 (2,163 were counted in a survey taken in 1577, but a gap of nearly two centuries makes extrapolation more than a little uncertain). But how far were they sticking to their brief? As late as 1604 Parliament was still insisting that the "ancient, true, and proper use" of an inn was the "receipt, relief, and lodging of wayfarers", and that inns should only be allowed to sell ale to other customers for an hour from noon. But there are strong suggestions that even in the late 14th century the distinction between inn and alehouse was becoming blurred, and that this blurring was the result of an administrative oversight.

The text of the London ale-conner's oath, contained in Letter Book D covering the years 1309-14, is as follows: *"Ye shal swere that ye shal wete no Brewer ne Brewster Hukster cook ne pibaker within your Warde that sillith owt of here hows a galon of the beste ale above 1½d a galon of the secund ale above 1d: ne otherwise than the mesur enselyd and ful of cler ale... And ye shall be redy to make your tast of ale anon whan ye be requirid by the brewer or brewster. And if ye know eny brewer that owtith eny ale before hit be tastid ... ye shall certefy all such to your aldermen... And for ... favour ne hate ne non other cause ye shal nat concele no brewer ne brewster hukster cook ne pibaker that doeth against eny poynte above seyd ne hem spare ne wrongfully..."* The inclusion of cooks and piebakers on the list may come as a surprise: presumably they were acting as hucksters in order to enhance the appeal of their own products, a pie and a pint being a much more attractive proposition than a pie by itself. The omission of innkeepers, however, is more significant, strongly implying that in the early 14th century innkeepers did not generally sell ale "out of here hows". But in the 1380s we begin to find hostellers such as that John Warner of Stockton, Wiltshire, cited by Judith M Bennett as the village's most frequent brewer, and Richard Goodfayre, lessee of the Crown, a substantial inn in Chiddingfold, Surrey, being presented for brewing out of the assize. The two cases are slightly different in that Warner started as a brewer and then became a victualler and hosteller while Goodfayre appears to have started as a hosteller and then began brewing for sale; but the inference from their cases is that the two of them ended up operating as both innkeepers and alehouse keepers, and that it was as brewers and alehouse keepers rather than as innkeepers that they were presented. In 1406, during Dick

Whittington's second term as Mayor, hostellers were specifically added to the formulaic list of those bound by the Assize and recorded in the London Letter Books as follows: "Also, whereas it had been formerly established that no brewer, hosteler, huckster, cook, or piebaker, should sell a gallon of best beer within their houses for more than 2d by marked measure, and outside their houses for more than 1½d, many nevertheless sell a gallon of best beer for 3d, 4d, and 5d, and by hanaps (unstamped mugs) and not by the gallon, potel, or quart duly sealed, and, further, they daily make and sell outside their houses for 1½d an inferior beer which they sell within their houses for 2d, contrary to the ordinance aforesaid. It was therefore ordained by the said Mayor and Aldermen that those found acting contrary to the said ordinance shall forfeit their beer and vessels and be committed to prison, the informer getting half of the forfeiture." The injunction was repeated, with the punishment reduced to a fine, in 1411, making it hard to escape the conclusion that by at least the early 15th century, and by implication earlier still, London innkeepers commonly opened their doors to local drinkers as well as to passing wayfarers.

London vintners operated as taverners from 1100 or earlier, and London alehouses were first recorded in 1212. Provincial towns and cities had wine taverns by the mid-13th century and alehouses from the mid-14th. By about the same time, inns had started opening their doors to the non-travelling public. Meanwhile, somewhere along the way, cooks and piebakers had routinely started selling ale to accompany their own offerings. It had been a long time coming, but by the early 15th century the pub had definitely arrived.

The Oldest Inns

But as this chapter started by asking which is the oldest pub in the country, it would not be fair to conclude without at least an attempt at an answer. But there have to be conditions – if only two of them. One is that the candidate must have been in continuous or near-continuous operation as a pub over the centuries; and the other is that a large part of the visible fabric must be original.

The first test rules out two of the least credible claimants, the Trip to Jerusalem and the Fighting Cocks; other candidates such as the Oxenham Arms at South Zeal in Devon also fail it (in this case, it was the manor-house of the Burgoyne family for many years after the Dissolution). There are, though, some that pass; but three that dare to lay claim to Saxon origin don't.

The "oldest" (according to the Guinness Book of Record) is the Bingley Arms at Bardsey, a suburb of Leeds: supposedly it was a "priests' inn" as early as 953. True, All Hallows Church in Bardsey contains much work from around 900 including England's oldest church tower. But it is not listed in the Domesday Book and probably, therefore, had no permanent priest until it was substantially extended in the late 12th century. A manse could have been part of the project, and the Bingley Arms might well have been it. In 1205 the manor was given to Kirkstall Abbey and was run as a grange – that is, with a farmhouse on the site in which a monk or a lay steward lived. The Bingley Arms might equally well have been that grange (although there is a much more modern house in the village called Bardsey Grange), to which the name "Priest's Inn" (in the other, older, sense of the word "inn", which is simply "house") might well have been attached. All these possibilities aside, though, the whole place appears to have been rebuilt in the 16th century, refronted in the 18th, and extended in the 19th. If there is any trace of Saxon stonework in its foundations, nobody has seen it for 500 years.

Next comes the Godbegot House in Winchester, a well-known inn on the Pilgrim's Way in the 14th century and almost certainly a monastic *hospitium* for centuries before that. Its provenance is that it was part of the manor of Godbegot granted to the remarkable Emma, daughter of Duke Richard of Normandy and wife of both Ethelred the Unready and Canute; that on her death in 1052 she bequeathed the manor to St Swithun's Abbey; and that what is now the Godbegot

House became its *hospitium*. It might be true, although it would be hard to prove; and the existing building is no earlier than mid-16th century with a range of outbuildings at the back that might just be a century older. In any case, it is no longer a hotel or even a pub, but is part of a national pizza and pasta chain.

The Grosvenor in Shaftesbury is the third claimant, having originally been (it is said) the guest-house of Shaftesbury Abbey, founded in 888 by Alfred the Great himself with his own sister as abbess, and the first all-female convent in England. (Previously, monks and nuns had lived side-by-side on the same site, albeit in different buildings). Again, it might well be true, for there was certainly an inn of the site at the time of the Dissolution; but in the 1820s the whole site was cleared and the present, and indeed very refined, Regency coaching inn was built as new.

If none of our very oldest claimants meets our conditions (the presence of the Bingley Arms in the Guinness Book of Records notwithstanding), where should we look next? The Ostrich at Colnbrook, under the Heathrow flight-paths, was donated as a hospice to Abingdon Abbey in 1106 by one Milo Crispin (or perhaps simply Sir Crispin, if "Milo" is a rendition of "*miles*" or knight). But for all its antique appearance, what you actually see (as is so often the case) dates only from around 1500. Exactly the same could be said of the Olde Bell at Hurley, Berkshire, *hospitium* of Hurley Priory since (possibly) 1135 but entirely replaced in the late 15th century and substantially altered since then. In fact it's surprising how few of the apparently ancient buildings that still dot our country lanes and high streets go back much further than 1550-ish, which marks the beginning of the 120-year period described by WG Hoskins (*The Rebuilding of Rural England*, 1953) as "the great rebuilding". This was a time of economic growth, rising expectations, and changing tastes, when those who could afford to completely replaced their medieval manor-houses (and inns) in various neo-classical sub-genres, while those who couldn't altered and extended theirs beyond recognition. At the same time the less durable dwellings of the poor, which were in a more or less permanent state of entropy anyway, were being replaced with cottages built of cheaper and longer-lasting brick. Examining the physical evidence of daily life before the 16th century thus becomes a branch not of the history of architecture but of archaeology.

The ambiguity (or complete lack) of early documentary evidence combined with this wholesale upgrading of the nation's real estate has made the "oldest pub" question as unanswerable as it is trivial. The quest for the oldest pub in England needn't end, though, in the inevitable failure to find a precise name, address, and postcode. What is more important is that there are a handful of places where it's just possible to get some sense of what a 14th-century hostelry might have looked and, to a limited extent, even felt like. Here are three: you may know more yourself. (There are many other verifiably 14th-century inns such as the Crown at Chiddingfold in Surrey; these are merely my very personal candidates for the most timeless and authentic atmosphere). To get the best out of them, whether your choices or mine, you need the talisman of hard fact to protect yourself against the charm of their myths, legends, and unsubstantiated claims. I would recommend a visit to www.britishlistedbuildings.co.uk before a visit to the pub itself.

The first and perhaps most obvious is the back yard of the George at Norton St Philip in Somerset, which has already been described above. Having a pint here, especially on a quiet day when there's no-one else around, is the closest experience I have ever had to being transported back to the Middle Ages. Its completeness and intimacy make it more atmospheric than any crumbling castle or grand cathedral.

Less obvious and, it has to be said, a good deal less atmospheric, is the Red Lion in Southampton High Street. Behind the fake half-timbered facade, though, is a genuine treasure of medieval vernacular architecture: a late 14th-century hall-house which has somehow avoided having a floor inserted. The tie-beam roof high above your head is actually 16th century as (of course) are the fireplaces. But the plan is original, as are many parts of the fabric including the solar in the east wing, the partition-screen, and the timbers supporting the gallery. And the vaulted Court Room, where in 1415 Henry V sentenced some rebellious barons on the eve of his departure for Agincourt, is older still – 12th century, it's thought.

My personal favourite, though, is another surviving hall-house. It's the Shaven Crown in Shipton-under-Wychwood, Gloucestershire; and apart from the jokey name (it was the plain Crown until quite recently, when some wag decided to contrive a pun on its monastic origin) it is perfect. We know the date of its original construction from the account books of Bruern Abbbey, which built it as a *hospitium* in 1384. It was, like everywhere else, somewhat remodelled in the 16th century; but the hall and courtyard survive intact, as does the solar. Despite its huge popularity (this is the Cotswolds, after all) it is still highly atmospheric and, to ice the cake, it has letting rooms, so you can not only enjoy a beer in the 14th century – you can sleep there, too.

APPENDIX 1: INN SIGNS AND WONDERS

Few aspects of the history of pubs and inns attract as much popular interest as the topic of names and signs – perhaps no surprise, given the surrealism displayed on so many pub signboards. It's hard for anyone, however incurious, to pass a Pig & Whistle or a Cat & Fiddle or a Shoulder of Mutton & Cauliflower without wondering what, if anything, the name might mean and how it came about. And ever since Larwood & Hotten's *History of Signboards* was first published in 1866 there's been no shortage of antiquarian authors eager to stretch and bend the evidence to breaking point to create plausible explanations. Forests have been felled and lakes of ink drained to propound theories ranging from the apparently scholarly to the simply absurd in a field where source material is so lacking as to make any enquiry wholly speculative. Fortunately the subject lies somewhat outside the scope of this book, which is why it has been consigned to the indignity of the appendices.

The earliest pub names I have come across belong to taverns and are either simply descriptive, like the Green Lattice in Bristol, recorded as early as 1241, or possessive, like Croxford's Tavern in Oxford recorded in 1285. The great age of inn signs when talents of the order of John Taylor, John Gay, and Joseph Addison considered the subject worthy of satire lies some centuries in the future. Nevertheless there are some sign-related issues affecting the late Medieval period, particularly as regards the alestake's role in enforcing the Assize of Bread and Ale, that need to be considered.

First, though, we need to rebut two of those ancient canards that have been blithely repeated so often that they are taken as solid historical fact when actually they have no foundation in the available evidence at all.

The first is that the oldest pub name of all is the Bush, either descending in unbroken line from Ancient Rome, where taverns were customarily designated by bunches of vine-leaves, or derived from the alestake itself with its prominent garland of leaves. For a start, there's nothing to suggest that Roman *thermopolia* were ever advertised by bunches of vine-leaves; and as we have already discovered there is no possibility of continuity in custom and practice between Roman and Medieval Britain anyway. Secondly, the alestake might not turn out to be as ancient as is commonly supposed. And finally, the Bush is not a particularly early pub name. The Bush at Morwenstow, Cornwall, may have some late Saxon fragments in its fabric, but has only been a pub called the Bush since the 16th century at the earliest. And the Vintners company has no trace of a bush in its coat of arms, which shows three tuns supported by swans.

The second and even greater canard, first perpetrated by Larwood & Hotten and now taken as Gospel, is that *titulus* 47 of the Bayeux Tapestry, "*Hic Domus Incenditur*", is evidence of alehouses in Saxon England because the building being fired by two Norman soldiers has an alestake. This is an error that could only be made by somebody who had never actually seen the tapestry. The building depicted is quite clearly a high-status dwelling – the hall of a local thegn, perhaps. It is of two storeys, with ground-floor timber uprights that boast decorated and perhaps even gilded plinths and capitals. The upper floor has an arched and apparently stone-cased dormer over polychrome bargeboards, while the roof is either tiled or shingled rather than thatched and has a little decorative pinnacle on each gable-end. The very broad sleeves on the dress of the woman fleeing the blaze indicate somebody of rank. And finally, on either wing of the building are two stubby carved finials, one of which might possibly be a dragon. It's these finials that Larwood & Hotten took for an alestake, which they resemble in no way whatever. In fact King Harold's own house (*titulus* 33) has almost identical finials – and no-one ever accused King Harold of running an alehouse! What actually happened was that William's army ravaged the districts around Pevensey to provoke Harold to come out and fight before his army had recovered from its forced march from York and before he could raise reinforcements – a strategy that proved entirely successful. Burning the halls of influential local dignitaries in Harold's own home county would put much heavier political pressure on him to respond before he was ready than firing peasant huts, whether they were "ale-houses" or not; and this is precisely what is being shown in *titulus* 47.

Besides, I have my doubts about the antiquity of the alestake. If ale was a household commodity not much traded in Anglo-Saxon England, except in port cities such as Chester and, of course, London, there would be no need to advertise its availability by raising the alestake. But even after the Conquest, when ale-selling became so widespread, why would anyone in a village of 30 or 40 households have needed to advertise? If word of mouth failed, the distinctive and pervasive smell of malt being mashed would have been evidence enough that someone was brewing and might have a surplus to sell. Even in a larger or more dispersed village a pole with a bunch of leaves attached would have been redundant, for the average brew was so small – typically 40 gallons – and the demand for ale so great – a gallon per person per day, supposedly – that each brew could easily have been presold, or possibly even brewed to order by private arrangement between neighbours.

Only when officialdom caught on to these transactions did an alestake become necessary. The onus was on the brewster to summon the aletaster; but the temptation, given the inevitable tolcester or alesilver or amercement, was towards concealment. The alestake – an odd (to our eyes) but very practical form of signpost in a community where even the priest might only have been semi-literate – was a symbol that what had once been private business was now public; and that whenever money changed hands the authorities were dutifully supervising and regulating the transaction. The alestake is therefore not a hangover from antiquity at all, and postdates rather than predates the appointment of ale-tasters from the late 12th century onward. (Incidentally, what the ale-taster would *not* do, once summoned, was pour a puddle of ale on to a bench and sit in it for a few minutes to see whether his leather breeches stuck to it. Heaven knows what the origin of this tale is; but it has become so widely accepted that in some municipalities where the office has been revived as a part of civic ceremonial the pantomime is acted out as solemnly as if it were the Mass. But the viscosity of ale is no guide to quality, merely an indication of how well-attenuated or fully-fermented it is. What the ale-taster was really looking out for was the sour off-flavour that betrayed spoilage and the thin body that betrayed weakness, and in this task he was better-served by his palate than his buttocks).

The question of inn signs is an entirely separate one. These evolved in a quite different context – that of the busy urban street where every craft traded under its own sign and where, to succeed, you had to shout louder than your competitors. Innkeepers, however, laboured under a peculiar disadvantage: they had no recognised trade sign. Their organised mistery was a comparative latecomer to the scene and boasted a peculiarly anonymous coat of arms. Its three barley sheaves might be easily confused with the bakers' three wheatsheaves; its supporters – white horses – and achievement – a ship under sail – were also far from unique. It also bore (and bears to this day) a crossed St Julian's Cross for its patron saint. A St Julian's Cross is doubled or "fitchee", with crosslets at either end of the transverse and across the head. Cross two of them diagonally and you have a trade sign that looks like nothing very much – certainly nothing as obvious as, say, a cutler's knife, and nothing that gives much of a clue to the business of the house to which it is attached.

To complicate matters further, each inn had its own history of ownership and therefore its own name. Those that had previously been *hospitia* might bear a religious sign such as the Lamb or the Angel. Those that had originally been townhouses might be distinguished by the armorial bearings of their former owners – the Bear & Ragged Staff for the Nevilles, say, or the Eagle & Child for the Stanleys. A third source of names and signs might be the arms of a new dynasty – a White Hart to prove the innkeeper's loyalty to Henry IV after the Lancastrian coup of 1399, or a White Lion to celebrate the Yorkist counter-coup of 1461. As literacy began to spread in the 16th century, the craft signs that denoted other trades gradually died out, so that today we are left only with the pawnbroker's three golden coins (bezants, not balls!) and the bloodied and bandaged barber-surgeon's pole. Inns and the alehouses that aspired to their social status kept their individual names and their pictorial signs – and have done so to this day.

APPENDIX 2: DE LUDIS

Sadly, we don't have as many word-pictures of medieval merry-making as we would like. One that we do possess is the section "*De Ludis*" from Fitzstephen's *Description of London* of about 1190, which was first published over 400 years later as an appendix to John Stow's *Survey of London*. The Londoners of Fitzstephen's day were evidently a lusty lot, enjoying mock combat, ice-skating, and a host of other full-blooded outdoor sports. Here, as much for entertainment as for education, is Stow's translation.

"Let us now proceed to the sports of the city; since it is expedient that a city be not only an object of utility and importance, but also a source of pleasure and diversion. Hence even in the seals of the chief pontiffs, up to the time of Pope Leo, there was engraved on one side of the Bull the figure of St Peter as a fisherman, and above him a key stretched out to him, as it were, from heaven by the hand of God, and around him this verse – "For me thou left'st thy ship, receive the key." On the obverse side was represented a city, with this inscription, Golden Rome. It was also said in praise of Augustus Caesar and the city of Rome, "All night it rains, the shows return with day, Caesar, thou bear'st with Jove alternate sway." London, instead of theatrical shows and scenic entertainments, has dramatic performances of a more sacred kind, either representations of the miracles which holy confessors have wrought, or of the passions and sufferings in which the constancy of martyrs was signally displayed.

Moreover, to begin with the sports of the boys (for we have all been boys), annually on the day which is called Shrovetide, the boys of the respective schools bring each a fighting cock to their master, and the whole of that forenoon is spent by the boys in seeing their cocks fight in the school-room. After dinner, all the young men of the city go out into the fields to play at the well-known game of foot-ball. The scholars belonging to the several schools have each their ball; and the city tradesmen, according to their respective crafts, have theirs. The more aged men, the fathers of the players, and the wealthy citizens, come on horseback to see the contests of the young men, with whom, after their manner, they participate, their natural heat seeming to be aroused by the sight of so much agility, and by their participation in the amusements of unrestrained youth.

Every Sunday in Lent, after dinner, a company of young men enter the fields, mounted on warlike horses – "On coursers always foremost in the race;" of which "Each steed's well-train'd to gallop in a ring." The lay-sons of the citizens rush out of the gates in crowds, equipped with lances and shields, the younger sort with pikes from which the iron head has been taken off, and there they get up sham fights, and exercise themselves in military combat. When the king happens to be near the city, most of the courtiers attend, and the young men who form the households of the earls and barons, and have not yet attained the honour of knighthood, resort thither for the purpose of trying their skill. The hope of victory animates everyone. The spirited horses neigh, their limbs tremble, they champ their bits, and, impatient of delay, cannot endure standing still. When at length "The charger's hoof seizes upon the course," the young riders having been divided into companies, some pursue those that go before without being able to overtake them, whilst others throw their companions out of their course, and gallop beyond them.

In the Easter holydays they play at a game resembling a naval engagement. A target is firmly fastened to the trunk of a tree which is fixed in the middle of the river, and in the prow of a boat driven along by oars and the current stands a young man who is to strike the target with his lance; if, in hitting it, he break his lance, and keep his position unmoved, he gains his point, and attains his desire: but if his lance be not shivered by the blow, he is tumbled into the river, and his boat passes by, driven along by its own motion. Two boats, however, are placed there, one on each side of the target, and in them a number of young men to take up the striker, when he first emerges from the stream, or when "A second time he rises from the wave." On the bridge, and in balconies on the banks of the river, stand the spectators, "well disposed to laugh."

During the holydays in summer the young men exercise themselves in the sports of leaping, archery, wrestling, stone-throwing, slinging javelins beyond a mark, and also fighting with bucklers. Cytherea leads the dances of the maidens, who merrily trip along the ground beneath the uprisen moon.

Almost on every holy day in winter, before dinner, foaming boars, and huge-tusked hogs, intended for bacon, fight for their lives, or fat bulls or immense boars are baited with dogs. When that great marsh which washes the walls of the city on the north side is frozen over, the young men go out in crowds to divert themselves upon the ice. Some, having increased their velocity by a run, placing their feet apart, and turning their bodies sideways, slide a great way: others make a seat of large pieces of ice like mill-stones, and a great number of them running before, and holding each other by the hand, draw one of their companions who is seated on the ice: if at any time they slip in moving so swiftly, all fall down headlong together. Others are more expert in their sports upon the ice; for fitting to, and binding under their feet the shinbones of some animal, and taking in their hands poles shod with iron, which at times they strike against the ice, they are carried along with as great rapidity as a bird flying, or a bolt discharged from a cross-bow. Sometimes two of the skaters having placed themselves a great distance apart by mutual agreement, come together from opposite sides; they meet, raise their poles, and strike each other; either one or both of them fall, not without some bodily hurt: even after their fall they are carried along to a great distance from each other by the velocity of the motion; and whatever part of their heads comes in contact with the ice is laid bare to the very skull. Very frequently the leg or arm of the falling party, if he chance to light upon either of them, is broken. But youth is an age eager for glory and desirous of victory, and so young men engage in counterfeit battles, that they may conduct themselves more valiantly in real ones.

Most of the citizens amuse themselves in sporting with merlins, hawks, and other birds of a like kind, and also with dogs that hunt in the woods. The citizens have the right of hunting in Middlesex, Hertfordshire, all the Chilterns, and Kent, as far as the river Cray."

APPENDIX 3: I WYLL YOW TELL A FULL GOOD SPORT

Sadly, there are very few literary portraits of Medieval alehouse customers other than Glutton and his friends in *Piers Plowman* and sundry defendants in court-cases. *I Wyll Yow Tell* from the mid-15th century is not perhaps truly representative in that it follows the female clientele of a wine-tavern and the vicissitudes of their relationships with men; but as it has not hitherto formed part of the usual canon of pub-related literature it is, I think, well worth reprinting in full.

> I wyll yow tell a full good sport
> How gossyps gather them on a sort
> Theyre syk bodies for to comfort,
> When thei mett in a lane ore stret.
>
> But I dare not, fore ther displeasaunce,
> Tell off thes maters half the substaunce;
> But yet sumwhatt off their governaunce,
> As fare as I dare, I will declare.
>
> Good gossipe myn, where have ye be?
> It is so long syth I yow see.
> Where is the best wyn? tell yow me.
> Can yow ought tell ful wele.
>
> I know a drawght off mery-go-downe,
> The best it is in all thys towne;
> But yet wold I not, fore my gowne,
> My husbond it wyst, ye may me trust.

Call forth yowr gossips by and by,
Elynore, Jone, and Margery,
Margaret, Alis, and Cecely;
For thei will come both all and sume.

And ich of them wyll sumwhat bryng,
Gosse, pygge, ore capons wyng,
Pastes off pigeons, ore sum other thyng;
For a galon of wyn thei will not wryng.

Go befoore be tweyn and tweyn,
Wysly, that ye be not seen;
Fore I must home, and come ageyn,
To witt i-wys where my husbond is.

A strype ore ii God myght send me,
If my husbond myght her se me.
She that is aferd, lett her fle,
Quod Alis than, I dred no man.

Now be we in tavern sett,
A drowght off the best lett hymn fett,
To bryng owr husbondes out off dett;
For we will spend, tyll God more send.

Ech off them brought forth ther dysch;
Sum brought flesh, and sume fysh.
Quod Margaret mek, now with a wysh,
I wold Ane were here, she wold make us chere.

How sey yow, gossips, is this wyne good?
That it is, quod Elenore, by the rood;
It cherisheth the hart, and comfort the blood;
Such jonckettes among shal mak us lyv long.

Anne, byd fill a pot of muscadell;
fore off all wynes I love it well,

Swete wynes kepe my body in hele;
If I had off it nought, I shuld tak gret thought.

How look ye, gossip, at the bordes end?
Not mery, gossip,? God it amend.
All shal be well, elles God it defend;
Be mery and glad, and sitt not so sadd.

Wold God I had done aftur yowr counsell!
Fore my husbond is so fell,
He betyth me lyk the devill off hell;
And the more I cry, the lesse mercy.

Alys with a lowd voyce spak then,
I-wis, she seid, lytyll good he cane,
That betyth ore strykyth ony woman,
And specially his wyff; God gyve him short lyve!

Margaret mek seid, So mot I thryffe,
I know no man that is alyffe,
That gyve me ii strokes, but he shal have fyffe;
I ame not aferd, though I have no berd.

On cast down her schott, and went her wey.
Gossip, quod Elenore, what dyd she paye?
Not but a peny. Lo, therefore I saie,
She shall be no more of owr lore.

Such gestes we may have i-nowe,
That will not fore ther shott alow.
With whom cum she? gossipe, with yow?
Nay, quod Jone, I come alone.

Now rekyn owr shott, and go we hence,
What? cost it ich of us but iii pence?
Parde, thys is but a smale expence,
Fore such a sort, and all but sport.

Torn down the street where ye cum owt,
And we will compasse rownd abowt.
Gossip, quod Anne, wht nedyth that dowt?
Yowr husbondes be plesyd, when ye be reisyd.

What so ever ony man thynk,
Whe cum fore nowght but fore good drynk
Now lett us go whom and wynk;
For it may be sen, where we have ben.

This is the thought that gossips tak,
Ones in the weke mery will thei mak,
And all small drynk thei will forsak;
But wyne of the best shall han no rest.

Sume be at the taverne ons in a weke;
And so be sume every daie eke;
Ore ellis thei will gron and make them sek.
Fore thynges usid will not be refusyd.

Who sey yow, women, is it not soo?
Yes, surely, and that ye wyll knowl;
And therfore lat us drynk all a row,
And of owr syngyng mak a good endyng.

Now fyll the cupe, and drynk to me;
And than shal we good felows be.
And of thys talkng leve will we,
And speak then good off women.

Further Reading

Peter Clark, *The English Alehouse: A Social History 1200-1830* (Longman, 1983).

Judith M Bennett, *Ale, Beer and Brewsters in England: Women's Work in a Changing World 1300-1600* (Oxford University Press, 1996).

Martyn Cornell, *Beer: The Story of the Pint* (Headline, 2003).

Ian Hornsey, *History of Beer and Brewing* (Royal Society of Chemistry 2003).

Tim Unwin, *Wine and the Vine* (Routledge, 1991).

Ted Bruning, *Golden Fire: The Story of Cider* (Bright Pen Books, 2012).

Ann Hagen, *Anglo-Saxon Food & Drink* (Anglo-Saxon Books, 2006).

Stephen Pollington, *The Mead-Hall* (Anglo-Saxon Books, 2003).

Rebecca Roseff, www.historyatthecidermuseum.org.uk/orchards (2007).

Louis Francis Salzman, *Industries of the Middle Ages* (1913).

Alicia Amherst, *A History of Gardening in England* (1895).

Frederick W Hackwood, *Inns, Ales and Drinking Customs of Old England* (1909).

Joseph Strutt, *Sports and Pastimes of the English People* (1801).

Colin Platt, *The English Medieval Town* (Secker & Warburg 1976).

Christopher Dyer, *Standards of Living in Late Medieval England* (Cambridge University Press 1989), and *Everyday Life in Medieval England* (Hambledon & London 1994).

Richard W Unger, *Beer in the Middle Ages and the Renaissance* (University of Pennsylvania Press 2004).

James Brown, *Villagers: 750 Years of Life in an English Village* (Amberley Publishing 2011).

JJ Jusserand, *English Wayfaring Life in the Middle Ages* (1884).

Pete Brown, *Shakespeare's Local* (Macmillan 2012).

Larwood & Hotten, *History of Signboards* (1866).

Rowland Parker, *The Common Stream* (Collins 1975)

INDEX

A

Adam & Eve
  Norwich · 108
æla huse · 53, 77, 79
Aelfric
  Colloquy · 16, 33, 34, 37, 53
ale · 11, 15, 16, 18, 19, 20, 21, 22, 23, 24, 25, 26, 27, 28, 29, 30, 31, 33, 35, 41, 44, 45, 46, 47, 51, 53, 56, 57, 58, 59, 63, 64, 65, 66, 72, 74, 76, 77, 80, 83, 84, 85, 86, 87, 89, 90, 93, 98, 99, 100, 105, 106, 108, 109, 112, 113, 114, 115, 117, 118, 123, 131, 138, 139, 146, 147
alehoof · 20, 26, 29
alehouse · 7, 52, 53, 54, 55, 59, 60, 61, 63, 64, 65, 84, 87, 88, 89, 90, 93, 94, 95, 98, 100, 102, 106, 109, 113, 114, 115, 117, 119, 120, 121, 122, 123, 125, 137, 138, 146, 153
alestake · 144, 145, 146
ale-stake · 58, 64
ale-taster · 58, 147
Alfred the Great · 70, 75, 141
Angel
  Guildford · 128
Angel & Royal
  Grantham · 129, 130
Angevins · 34
apples · 34, 42, 43, 47
assize · 22, 57, 59, 65, 84, 85, 93, 96, 118, 138
Assize of Bread and Ale · 58, 64, 144
Athelstan · 71

B

barley · 20, 23, 25, 58, 113, 147
Battle of Maldon · 37
Bayeux Tapestry · 145
Bede
  the Venerable · 50, 51, 70, 78
Bede, the Ven · 32
beekeeping · 38, 40
beer · 16, 24, 26, 27, 28, 29, 30, 44, 45, 53, 59, 63, 72, 82, 85, 99, 113, 114, 139, 143
bees · 37
beor · 44, 45, 72
beorscipe · 51, 78
Beowulf · 37, 50, 72
Beton the Brewster · 88, 98, 137
Bingley Arms
  Leeds · 140
Black Death · 22, 61, 64, 107, 111, 114, 115, 116, 117, 121, 132
Boar's Head
  Southwark · 134
Bordeaux · 34, 46
boroughs · 56, 57, 115
braciatores · 84, 88, 113
braggot · 26
Brewers' Company · 84
brewsters
  brewster · 22, 25, 26, 57, 58, 59, 61, 64, 65, 66, 86, 113, 115, 123
Bush
  Farnham · 128
  Morwenstow · 145

C

Caedmon · 50, 51, 78

159

caepælepel · 78, 79
Cambridge · 8, 35, 39, 112, 157
cambuca · 62, 119
Canterbury · 32, 36, 39, 46, 49, 69, 79, 89, 127
Canterbury Tales · 36
Canute · 71
Carta Mercatoria · 36
Caxton
    William · 43
ceap · 71, 74, 76
ceapælepel · 76
cellis vinariis venalia · 80, 82
Chaucer
    Geoffrey · 36, 37, 41, 64, 88, 94, 121, 126, 128
Chester · 49, 52, 56, 113, 146
chopyn · 89
churches · 32, 54, 55, 71, 108, 118
cider · 31, 34, 42, 43, 44, 45, 46, 47
Cock
    Gamlingay · 99, 118
Columella · 38
coquina · 80, 82
Crown
    Chiddingfold · 138
Croxford's
    Oxford · 108
curfew · 90, 91, 92, 115, 135

D

Domesday · 21, 34, 39, 52, 83, 107, 140
drinking at pins · 72, 78

E

Edgar · 32, 52, 55
Edward I · 36, 91, 119, 126, 135
Edward II · 36, 103, 126, 127, 130
Edward IV · 120
Edward the Confessor · 39
Edward the Elder · 70, 71
emmer · 20, 25
Ethelred the Unready · 39, 53, 71, 74, 77, 103, 140

F

fairs · 35, 60, 105, 107, 124
Fighting Cocks
    St Albans · 123
Fitzstephen
    William · 23, 24, 80, 82, 87, 149
football · 12, 62, 119
Foxton
    Cambridgeshire · 118, 120

G

Gascony · 34, 46, 112
Geoffrey of Monmouth · 88, 124
George
    Norton St Philip · 40, 129, 130, 142
Gilbert de Mordone · 90, 117, 137
gill · 89
Glastonbury · 32
Glutton · 98, 99, 137, 153
Godbegot
    Winchester · 128, 140
Golden Cross
    Oxford · 108
Gow
    John · 93, 94, 95, 97
Green Lattice
    Oxford · 108
Grosvenor
    Shaftesbury · 141
guild · 12, 73, 84, 135, 136, 137

H

Hackwood

Frederick · 48, 49, 67, 157
Harry Bailey · 36, 126, 128, 136
Henry Fitz Ailwin · 86
Henry II · 23, 34, 36, 46, 124
Henry III · 103, 105
Henry VII · 120
Henry VIII · 121
Heorot · 50
herb bennet · 26
herbergour · 132
Hero of Alexandria · 43
hippocras · 40
Hobbes
   Thomas · 9, 10
Holy Days of Obligation · 11
honey · 19, 20, 21, 26, 27, 31, 37, 38, 39, 40, 41, 45, 81
hops
   hop · 16, 20, 24, 26, 27, 28, 29, 30
hospitia · 64, 126, 127, 128, 129, 133, 148
hospitium
   hospitia · 23, 125, 126, 129, 131, 140, 141, 143
hosteller · 117, 128, 132, 134, 136, 138
Houghton-cum-Wyton · 106, 107, 108
hucksters · 60, 72, 85, 138
Hydromellum · 38

I

I Wyll Tell Yow a Full Good Sport · 101
inn signs · 147
Inns of Chancery · 133, 134, 137
Inquisitio de nocte vagantibus · 91, 119, 135

J

Juvenal · 68

K

Kelmeston · 60, 66, 108
kindred group · 50, 73
kindred hall · 53, 54, 55, 77
Knights Hospitallers · 125

L

Langland
   William · 16, 60, 64, 85, 88, 98, 99, 109, 115, 121
Larwood & Hotten · 144
licentia · 87
London · 16, 28, 29, 33, 35, 46, 49, 67, 70, 71, 72, 74, 76, 77, 78, 80, 81, 83, 84, 85, 86, 88, 90, 93, 94, 95, 98, 100, 101, 109, 110, 112, 113, 115, 117, 128, 132, 133, 134, 135, 136, 137, 138, 139, 146, 149, 157
London Lickpenny · 100

M

Magna Carta · 57
malt · 17, 18, 24, 25, 28, 42, 45, 55, 65, 85, 146
mansiones · 48, 49
markets · 60, 105, 107
Martial · 68, 76, 108
Matthew the Tanner · 105, 109
mead · 15, 31, 37, 38, 39, 40, 41, 42, 72
meadowsweet · 19, 20, 29
Medieval Warm Period · 103
melomel · 41
mercatorium · 90
merchants · 18, 29, 33, 35, 36, 71, 72, 73, 74, 77, 81, 82, 83, 94, 105, 130, 131, 132, 133, 134
metheglyn · 40
Miller's Tale · 41, 94

161

Mirour de l'Omme · 93
monasteries · 32
morat · 41
mulsum · 38
muscadell · 102

N

New Inn
　Gloucester · 129, 130, 131
nightwalkers · 91, 92, 94, 97, 135
Norfolk · 46, 50, 111, 119, 125, 134
Norman Conquest · 20
Normandy · 34, 39, 46, 140
Normans · 21, 33, 34, 45, 46, 63, 81, 83

O

oats · 23, 25, 58
Offa of Mercia · 74
Olde Bell
　Hurley · 141
Ostrich
　Colnbrook · 141
Oswald of Northumbria · 53
Oxenham Arms
　South Zeal · 140
Oxford · 7, 22, 39, 58, 83, 93, 108, 109, 110, 113, 127, 131, 144, 157

P

Paternoster Row · 97
Peasants' Revolt · 121
piebakers · 85, 138, 139
Piers Plowman · 16, 64, 85, 89, 98, 115, 137, 153
piment · 40, 41
Plantagenet · 46, 57
Pliny the Elder · 19, 38, 43
potationes · 72, 78, 79

Pytheas of Massilia · 19

R

Rectitudines Singularum Personum · 38
Red Lion
　Southampton · 142
Regino of Prüm · 76
regrators · 60, 85
Rhenish · 95
Richard I · 57
Richard II · 40
Richard III · 129
Robin Hood · 121
Rose the Regrator · 85
Rouen · 29, 30, 34, 83
Rummer · 108

S

scot-ales · 55, 62
scotallae · 87, 93
screw-press · 43
sester · 39, 57
Shaven Crown
　Shipton-under-Wychwood · 143
Simony and Covetousness · 110
Snow
　John · 16
Southwark · 30, 36, 70, 82, 86, 87, 128, 133, 134, 137
Spread Eagle
　Midhurst · 125
St Augustine · 31, 70
St Dogmael's
　Ceredigion · 119
St Dunstan · 55, 72, 78, 79
St Ives · 105, 106, 108
St Paul's · 23, 25, 33
stallage · 107
Statute of Labourers · 111
Stockton · 118

162

Stourbridge Common · 35
Survey of London · 80, 149
sweet gale · 26, 29

T

Tabard
    Southwark · 36, 126, 128, 133
tabernae · 60, 68, 93
tabernae ecclesiasticae · 60
tabernarius · 76
taberni vinorum · 93
tabernus · 60, 76, 77
tavern · 54, 60, 67, 68, 74, 75, 76, 79, 80, 88, 91, 94, 95, 97, 98, 101, 102, 108, 110, 115, 119, 122, 153, 154
taverner · 82, 91, 92, 94, 95, 97, 101
taverns · 48, 75, 76, 78, 79, 80, 82, 83, 84, 88, 91, 92, 93, 94, 95, 96, 97, 100, 105, 108, 119, 123, 135, 139, 144, 145
The Forme of Cury · 40
The Ruin · 69, 73
The Vintry · 81, 83
thermopolia · 48, 49, 67, 73, 145
Thornbury · 115
tipplers · 113
Trip to Jerusalem
    Nottingham · 123
Tunning of Eleanour Rumming · 101

U

Upper Thames Street · 82

V

vineyards · 32
vintners · 35, 36, 80, 94, 106, 139
Virgil · 38
viticulture · 31, 32, 34, 75

W

Walsingham · 127
Walter of Henley · 104
West Stow · 50, 51
Wey Hill · 35
wheat · 20, 23, 25, 58, 110, 125
William of Malmesbury · 52, 72, 78, 82
William the Conqueror · 56, 103
wine · 16, 19, 23, 24, 31, 32, 33, 34, 35, 36, 37, 38, 39, 40, 41, 42, 43, 44, 46, 57, 67, 68, 71, 72, 76, 82, 83, 84, 88, 93, 94, 95, 97, 104, 108, 109, 112, 119, 124, 131, 139, 153
Worshipful Company of Innholders · 136
Wye · 46, 60, 115

Y

Y Goddodin · 37
yeast · 17, 18, 25, 27, 45
Yorkshire · 32